W9-DCH-462

GRANDMA'S

FRONT PORCH

Best always

Jam Varanese

©2008 JANE M. BODE CARACCI

ISBN: 978-0-9827442-8-4

All rights reserved. Please do not participate in or encourage piracy of copyrighted materials in violation of the author's rights. Purchase only authorized editions.

This is a work of fiction. Names, characters, places, and incidents either are the product of the author's imagination or are used fictitiously, and any resemblance to actual persons, living or dead, businesses, companies, events, or locales is entirely coincidental.

This book or parts hereof, may not be reproduced, stored in or introduced into a retrieval system or transmitted in any form or by any means electronic, mechanical, photocopying, recording or otherwise. It may not be translated without prior written permission of both the copyright holder and the publisher of the book.

First Edition

Fiction Publishing, Inc.
Ft. Pierce, Florida 34982
fictionpub@bellsouth.net

GRANDMA'S FRONT PORCH

JANE M. BODE CARACCI

DEDICATION

This book is dedicated to my
husband, Joe
for his understanding,
patience,
and constant love and
encouragement.

DEDICATION

This book is dedicated to my
husband, Joe
for his understanding,
patience,
and constant love and
encouragement.

ACKNOWLEDGEMENT

Special thanks to Diane DesRochers
for her time, friendship and trust.
Her help made it all possible.

Many thanks to Fort Pierce Writers
Group
I thank all for listening.

CHAPTER ONE

Slowly the front door opened, followed by the squeaky wood-framed screen door. An old lady in a faded cotton housedress covered with a well-worn apron, let the door shut behind her. She shuffled across the front porch and sat in a wicker rocker, easing herself onto the faded cushion. You could almost sense her deep sigh as she systematically rocked back and forth, looking straight ahead.

There are only four or five residential streets in Riversedge. This house is one of many built in the late thirties on a dead-end street in a small central North Carolina town just ten miles from the border of South Carolina. The town is past its prime and most residents have long since moved to greener pastures. The once freshly painted clapboard houses are now weather-worn, but most folks on tree-lined Turner Street work hard to keep their homes and yards neat and clean. Oh yes, there's one who parks his car on the front lawn and another has a rusty old washing machine on the back porch. But over the years, prejudices lessened and the community became interracial. Main Street, located in the middle of town, once the thriving centerpiece of Riversedge, now has several vacant stores and the few still in existence struggle to stay open. Main Street ends at the river's edge in a small park where a rusted statue of Robert E. Lee is its focal point. A few dilapidated wooden benches face the water but they are seldom used.

The town belongs to the past. The townspeople know that seven miles to the north is a modern town with banks, supermarkets, a post office and even a Wal-Mart, but something holds them to Riversedge, most having lived there a good part of their lives. Fort Bragg is fifty miles to the east so a couple of military families live here but come and go as their orders dictate.

People don't live on Turner Street long before they suspect a secret lurks behind some of the closed doors where appear unexplained happenings. Unable to put a finger on a reasonable explanation, suspicions rise and cause much speculation. With amateur sleuthing the mystery is bound to unravel sooner rather than later.

CHAPTER TWO

Tom and Sally Lester moved to Riversedge shortly after Tom reported for active duty at Fort Bragg. He commuted the fifty miles at first but it wasn't long before he was sent overseas. It was a difficult time for the couple. Sally was pregnant with their second child and hadn't met many people in their new surroundings. Tom wanted her to go north to where she lived before they were married. She'd have her Dad and friends close by, but Sally couldn't bear the thought of moving again, especially in her condition. So before Tom left for overseas, his sergeant who knew their situation, made arrangements for Sally and Tom to meet his mother, Mary Clarkson, who also lived in Riversedge. She was a delightful lady and only too glad to help. The Lester's liked her immediately as she did them. Their son, Tommy also liked her, calling her Nanny. Tom's departure was a sad time but he was confident his wife was a strong capable lady and would be well looked after.

When Sally delivered a beautiful baby girl, Nanny was a god-send, staying with Tommy for a few days after Sally brought baby Jenny home. Unfortunately, their friendship was short-lived because Mary had previous plans to move. To this day, the Lester's are in touch with Nanny.

Sally slowly became acquainted with her neighbors, but didn't develop any close friendships. Although lonely, she kept busy with the new baby and Tommy. One afternoon she took the kids for a walk. Four-year-old Tommy rode his tricycle while Sally pushed Jenny in her carriage. They hadn't gone far when Sally noticed an elderly woman sitting on her front porch. Eager to show off her new baby even though she'd heard rumors that the woman wasn't very friendly, they approached the house.

Tommy was a little distance ahead. "Tommy, turn the bike around and come back," Sally called. At the same time, she waved to the old woman. "Good afternoon, it's such a lovely day isn't it?" Immediately the woman stood up. She nodded. My heavens, Sally wondered, is she going to come and see the baby? But no, the old woman hurried into her house and soon was out of sight.

The little family continued their walk but Sally couldn't figure out the old woman. Somehow she felt sorry for her and wondered if she was lonely. The whole incident was just plain strange.

After the children were fed and having their afternoon nap, Sally went out on her front porch to write a letter to her husband Tom. His Army Reserve unit had been called up for active duty and four months later he was overseas. Tom was heartbroken not being able to be home for baby Jenny's birth but Sally sent him pictures of both Tommy and Jenny frequently.

Talk about lonely. Sally missed Tom and longed to be in his arms, making love and feeling the warmth of his body next to hers. Tears welled in her eyes but reality took over as Mr. Jacobs, the postman came up the steps. "Got a letter from your man Mrs. Lester and I bet you have one for him."

"Oh, yes, I just sealed and stamped it."

"I bet with a kiss." Mr. Jacobs smiled.

"Many kisses and with all my love."

"Are you alright?" he asked, noticing tears in her eyes, "and the little ones are okay?"

"Oh, I'm fine but Tommy doesn't understand where his Dad is

and why we have this crying thing instead of Daddy. It's hard on everyone, really."

"Well, you know if there's anything you need or I can do, all you have to do is ask," the postman said as he went down the stairs.

"Thank you so much. By the way do you know the name of that lady everyone calls Grandma?"

"I know who you mean, but I don't know her name because she never gets mail delivered to her house."

"What? You're kidding me. But she must at least have bills even if no one writes to her."

"I'm sure she does. I figure the bills and stuff like that are sent to another address, perhaps to a relative. I really don't know, but I guess that's the way she wants it. Now I'd best be on my way to deliver the mail to those who do want it. Bye for now."

Sally sat for a while and decided there was no figuring the woman, but she was certainly a strange one. Soon she heard little Jenny crying. She rushed upstairs to her. It was too early for Tommy to wake up from his nap so she brought Jenny outside and fed her a bottle. It wasn't long before the baby was again fast asleep cradled in her mother's arms. Sally closed her eyes and hummed a lullaby as her thoughts drifted to Jenny's Daddy. When he sees his beautiful little girl, it will be a wonderful day.

"Oh, my dear, how are you and that precious little baby?"

Startled at first, Sally answered, "Good afternoon, Mrs. Trundale."

"Can I come up and take a peek at the baby?

"Of course, do come and join us."

Mrs. Trundale was the Lester's next door neighbor. She's a nice lady, thought Sally although a bit nosey.

Her husband had died shortly before Tom and Sally moved to Riversedge. Like Sally, Mrs. Trundale was lonely. It was nice to chat with her once in a while. Also, if anyone knew anything about Grandma, Mrs. Trundale would. She'd lived here for many years.

"Why don't I put the baby back in her crib. She's sound asleep now. Then I'll get us a glass of ice tea. Quiet moments are so few and far between, let's enjoy them." Sally left but came back soon with a tray of ice tea and cookies and placed them on the table between the two rockers. They enjoyed small talk and after a while Sally asked, "Mrs. Trundale, I was wondering about the elderly lady everyone calls Grandma…umm, I do feel funny calling her Grandma. What is her name?"

Rose Trundale paused, rolled her eyes and said, "Oh my dear, my dear Sally, don't worry your head about that woman. Yes, everyone calls her

Grandma but I can't tell you her real name. I would if I knew but I don't and Sally pleeease do call me Rose."

"Alright, Rose. How long have you lived here?" Sally asked cautiously, feeling Rose was becoming annoyed.

"Well, let me see," she paused. "I guess it's about thirteen years now."

"And you still don't know that woman's name?"

"No, and I suspect no one on Turner Street does either. To tell you the truth, I really don't care. She's the most unfriendly, nasty old lady I ever did meet."

"Really, she doesn't seem to bother anyone."

"She bothers me. Don't you think it's a problem when someone doesn't even say hello to you? That bothers me a great deal."

CHAPTER THREE

At Wal-Mart one day, Sally noticed an attractive young woman at the next checkout line who looked vaguely familiar. It took a few minutes before she realized it was the same lady she occasionally saw on Turner Street. The women reached the exit at the same time. "Excuse me, but don't you live in Riversedge on Turner Street?" Sally asked.

"Yes, I was about to ask you the same thing."

"I'm Sally Lester. I live at the end of the street."

"So nice to meet you Sally, I'm Annie Wilson. I've seen you walking with your children. I noticed you had a little boy and a baby. How old is your son?"

"Tommy is four and baby Jenny is five months."

"My little guy is almost five."

"For heaven's sake, I didn't even know you had children. What I mean is I've never seen your son." Sally stumbled over her words. "What's his name?"

"Peter, and he's four but will be five in a couple of months."

Tommy was restless and Jenny was beginning to fuss so Sally said, "We'll definitely have to get together sometime with the kids. Annie, please do stop by for a cup of tea."

"I work at the Textile Factory three days a week, but I'd love to stop by someday."

"Do make that someday soon."

They went their separate ways. Sally couldn't help but notice Annie's sad eyes and hesitation but looked forward to seeing her again.

The weather turned warmer and soon the azalea bushes and magnolia trees were in full bloom. Sally's back yard was picture perfect with beautiful flowers she had planted. She enjoyed gardening and loved spending time outdoors with her children. It also helped pass the time. Several weeks passed since Sally met Annie and she wondered why she hadn't heard from her. For that matter she hadn't even seen her in the neighborhood. Maybe I'll take a walk down to her house to say hello. Remembering that Annie said she worked three days a week, Sally had no idea what days they were. Maybe it wasn't a good idea after all. Oh what the heck, she said to herself. She got the kids ready and off they went.

There were no signs of life when they got to Annie's house but she knocked on the front door anyway. She heard footsteps inside and waited. Then there wasn't a sound. She decided to forget it and turned to leave. Suddenly the door opened and there stood a huge man, a hairy man, his arms a mass of black hair and hair spilling over the top of his undershirt.

"What do yah want?" he asked in gruff voice.

Sally assumed it was Annie's husband even though she never saw him other than coming and going in his pickup truck. After a few seconds of silence Sally managed to say, "I'm a friend of Annie's, is she home?"

"Nah, she's at work," he grumbled.

"I'm sorry to bother you. Would you tell her Sally was here, that's me, I live down the street."

She no sooner got the words out than he said, "Yeah," and slammed the door shut.

As she hurried down the steps with a shiver, she saw Grandma directly across the street, sitting on her porch. Sally knew she had seen her so she waved. Well, if Grandma had seen them you would never have known as she just kept rocking back and forth, staring. Sally couldn't imagine at what.

That night after the children were down for the night, Sally sat on the front porch to relax and enjoy the evening breeze. It was dusk and lamp lights could be seen in the windows along Turner Street. She noticed there were no lights in Annie's house, but just then a car stopped in front of the house. Annie got out of the passenger's side and the car drove off. Her driver quickly rounded the dead-end. Sally couldn't see clearly, but caught a glimpse of what looked like a male driver. And Annie didn't go in the front but rather walked to the back of the house and out of sight. No sooner had Sally seen the lights turn on, when the house became dark again.

A truck that was kept in the back yard left and was quickly out of sight. It was too dark for Sally to make out who was in the truck. It didn't matter much anyway.

She sat in the dark waiting and hoping Tom would phone but no call came. She hadn't heard from him in over two weeks. Not hearing from him gave her a sinking feeling in the pit of her stomach. She finally went inside and sat by the phone for some time. As hard as she tried not to, the horrors of war took control of her thoughts. She got up and turned on the TV. Nothing interested her. She picked up her book but couldn't concentrate. Then, taking a sweater from the coat rack she turned off the porch lights and went back outside. There she sat in the dark. Tears fell as she prayed. "Oh God, please keep my Tom safe. I miss him so much."

It was quite late before Sally felt sleepy. She realized that all of the houses on Turner Street were pitch dark, except for Grandma's house. There was a light on in a back room. Sally hoped all was well with the old woman. At that moment, she saw two figures walk past the lit window. Who is in there with her, Sally wondered or was she imagining she saw someone?

CHAPTER FOUR

The door opened only as far as the chain lock would allow. Sally wasn't sure who was behind the door until she heard Annie ask, "Who is it?"

"Annie. It's Sally, Sally Lester. We met at Wal-Mart some time ago, remember?"

"Oh, oh yes," she said as she unhooked the lock and opened the door. There stood a very sad looking Annie, clothed in a worn bathrobe, her hair in a pony tail and wearing sunglasses. "Come in Sally."

"No, I have the children in the stroller out front." Annie came outside and the two women sat on the front stoop. "I just wanted to talk to you about a Halloween party I'm planning. Something simple, but some fun for the kids."

"That sounds great."

"There aren't any children down my end of the street so I was wondering if you know of any children at this end?"

'There's a little girl a few houses near the corner and I've seen two little ones across the street, maybe a house or two from the lady who's always sitting on her front porch. You might ask her what house they actually live in."

"Are you kidding, Grandma doesn't talk to anyone."

"She's your Grandma?"

Sally laughed. "No, no that's just what everyone around here calls her. No one seems to know her real name, at least I haven't heard of anyone who does."

"Really?"

"Yeah, but you know Annie, I just might ask her. I've often wondered if anyone ever even bothered to try and talk to the old lady. I certainly never saw anyone.

Yes, Annie I will. I really will," Sally said obviously trying to convince herself that is was a good idea. She then asked if Peter was home.

Annie's demeanor changed immediately. She became tense, withdrawn and sad. "Peter stays with my parents during the week and I bring him home on the weekend."

"It must be nice to have your parents close by."

"Well, it certainly helps with my working and I'm grateful having them nearby. Plus Sam, my husband, lost his job so he's busy out looking for work." Having said that, Annie stood and Sally knew it was time to leave.

"It's best I get going but I'll be in touch with you soon about the party."

"Sally, thank you," Annie said as she shut the door.

Instead of going directly to home Sally decided to cross the street. There was no one sitting on Grandma's front porch now, which puzzled Sally because while she and Annie were outside she saw her there on the porch. Sally was adamant, crossed the street, climbed the steps and rang Grandma's doorbell. She became nervous while waiting for the door to open. She wanted to disappear and began to think this wasn't such a good idea after all. But finally the door did open and Grandma stood there with a stern look on her face, "What do you want?" she asked sharply.

Sally took a deep breath, her knees shaking."I'm sorry to bother you, but could you possibly tell me which house near yours have two children living there? I'd like to invite them to a little Halloween Party."

It seemed like forever before the old woman answered "NO" and shut the door. Sally stood there stunned, not knowing what to do, feeling scared, angry and disappointed all at once. Slowly she went down the stairs. "Missy, missy the house number is two four six," Sally heard Grandma's voice and turned quickly only to see the door close again.

That night after the little ones were settled, Sally received her long awaited call from Tom. He couldn't talk long but asked about the kids then told her how much he loved her and wanted to be near her, to touch her naked body and to make love to her again and again. Sally's heart beat fast, tears rolling down her cheeks. She told Tom of her longings and love. In minutes the call was over and Sally felt alone again and unfulfilled. She held the phone close to her for a long time, thinking of Tom, wondering how much longer he'd be gone. "Damn this war," she yelled into the phone's dial tone.

Her thoughts shifted to the strange place where she lived, with so many unanswered questions. Annie so sad, such a beautiful woman and yet she looked pitiful. Then there's Grandma. Sally still couldn't believe she told her the house number. Why was she so cold but changed her mind and gave me the answer, Sally wondered, not being able to figure the old woman out. She thanked God she didn't have all these complications in her own life. On the other hand was she complicating her life by getting involved?

She sat there dreaming of what life would be like when Tom came home before realizing it was nearly midnight. It had been raining hard for some time. She opened the front door and stepped outside. It was pitch black. She stood for a minute or two and as she turned to go back inside she noticed the light was on in Grandma's back window. And again she saw the shadows of two people.

CHAPTER FIVE

During the next couple of weeks Sally met the Andersons who lived down the block from Annie and their daughter Meghan, as well as the Collin's children, six year-old Luke and four year-old Molly who lived in house number two-forty-six. She delivered their invitations for Halloween and both Moms volunteered to help make goodies. The week before the party, Sally busied herself making an army uniform costume for Tommy, baking cupcakes and making decorations.

The big day came and the kids really enjoyed themselves, playing games, eating and generally running all around the back yard, making lots of noise. Of course Rose came over to see what was going on and joined the group. The mommies got to know one another, sharing some of their life stories. All in all, the day was a great success. When everyone left, exhausted Sally cleaned up and put her children to bed after a very small snack.

Sally had just sat down on the porch when she heard, "Sally, dear Sally what a lovely little party. I do hope you didn't mind me joining in." This time Sally rolled her eyes and sighed. She wasn't up to Rose. She was the last person she wanted to talk to but being polite, answered, "Of course not Rose, come sit a minute." Sally got up from her chair but didn't invite Rose up on the porch. Rather, she just sat on the front steps. Rose preferred to stand and quickly got to the point of why she was really stopping by.

"Sally, someone told me they saw you talking to Grandma. Is that true?"

"Really, when was that?"

"Oh, I don't know, they didn't say."

"I really don't know what *they* are talking about."

"Then it's not true?"

At that, Sally knew Rose would not be satisfied until she got to the bottom of the story. "Rose, I asked Grandma a question. She answered and that was the total of our conversation. Period. I don't know what you heard but that was the extent of my talking to Grandma." Sally couldn't help adding, "not that it's anyone's business."

"Oh my dear, I agree but you know that woman is sick and I wouldn't want you to get hurt. You're such a sweet thing."

"I can't see how she would hurt me." Then Sally lied, "she was very lovely to me. Rose I'm sorry, I'm afraid I must go in now. I still have some cleaning up to do."

"I'd be glad to help," offered Rose.

"Oh, that won't be necessary. I just have to put things away and truthfully, I'm tired. I plan on getting to bed early. Thanks anyway." Sally turned and went up the steps and into the house. She knew Rose was not a happy camper but Sally really didn't care at that point. *And who the heck told her I was there anyway?* Somehow Sally had a sneaking suspicion it was Rose who saw her on Grandma's front porch, not somebody.

Over time it became obvious to Sally that when Annie was home, the truck was gone but when Annie was at work the truck was in the back yard. Sally presumed Sam only looked for work when Annie wasn't home, so she carefully picked her times to visit with Annie. This particular day Sally rang the doorbell. No one answered so she walked around to the back. Annie was taking clothes off the line. She called, "Annie," startling the woman.

"I can't talk to you now, please leave," Annie said without turning.

"Is everything alright?"

"Yes, but please, I'll talk to you later." With that Annie ran to the back door with the clothes in her arms, making sure they covered her face. For some time Sally suspected there was something very wrong in the Wilson household. She had the uneasy feeling Annie was being abused, both physically and verbally. Although she didn't see Annie that often, she did feel a connection even though the opportunity to become real friends never presented itself.

It was only a few days later when Annie was at Sally's front door, shaking, tears streaming down her cheeks.

"Annie what's the matter? Come in."

"I'm sorry to bother you."

"Don't be silly," said Sally.

"It's Peter, my little Peter is missing."

"What? Missing from where?"

"I can't find him anywhere. I went out back to hang clothes. He was in the living room watching his Saturday morning shows. I wasn't outside more than five minutes." By this time Annie was hysterical.

Sally put her arms around her friend and asked, "Is your husband home?"

"No."

"Is he at work? Can you reach him by phone?"

Sam isn't working and I have no idea where to reach him. He didn't come home last night. We went to pick up Peter at my parents. He dropped us off and left to go meet up with some of his drinking buddies. I haven't heard from him since."

"Could he have come by the house and picked up Peter while you were in the back?"

"God, no, I would have heard that damn truck. It's so loud. It's just not like Peter to go anywhere on his own."

Sally knew Annie was frantic. "Go home, Annie, take a deep breath and wash your face with cold water. "I'll ask Rose to come and babysit my kids. They're napping now."

Afterward she went to Annie's and when they were certain Peter wasn't hiding someplace in the house; closets, under beds, behind doors, all the places little kids love to hide, they took to the street. Somebody must have seen Peter.

Sally crossed the street and started ringing doorbells while Annie did the same on her side. Sally found Luke Collins playing in front of his house. She asked, "Luke have you seen Peter this afternoon?"

Luke shook his head and said, "Not since Halloween."

"If you do, tell your Mom to let Peter's Mom know, okay?" Sally started to the next house when she heard Sam's truck turn onto Turner Street.

CHAPTER SIX

S am's truck, and it was very loud, entered Turner Street at its usual fast clip, jumped the curb and drove to the back yard. Once he was in the house you could hear doors slam and Sam curse. In short order the truck started up again and sped towards the street. But just before he reached the curb he saw Annie running towards him.

He yelled at her. "You bitch you're out running around the street with the house wide open. What the hell are you doing?"

"Sam, Sam, Peter's missing, I'm looking for..." She didn't get a chance to finish.

Sam got out of his truck and grabbed Annie by the arm. "How can Peter be missing? Oh, with you running around the streets, I guess it's no wonder. What kind of mother are yah?" Sam tried to push Annie into the truck. She wouldn't get in. They struggled, he yelling, "You damn bitch, get in the truck if you know what's good for you." She didn't budge. He then gave her one hard slap across the face. She fell to the ground.

By this time neighbors were opening their doors to see what the commotion was. Grandma was standing on her porch across the street. Sam gave her one look, shook his fist at her and yelled, "What are you looking at you fat ass?"

Grandma didn't move a muscle. She just stood there. Sam cursed at her again, jumped in the truck leaving Annie lying on the ground. He sped down the street out of sight.

When Sally was about to go to the house next to Grandma's she saw Sam drive from his back yard. Like everyone else, she stopped to see what all the shouting was about. Her heart sank as she watched him smack Annie. At first she was stunned.

Ralph Barner, who lived a couple houses from the Wilsons ran to Annie who was still on the ground. He helped her up and brought her back to his house. She was like a broken doll.

As Mr. Barner was helping Annie to her feet Sally ran across the street. "Annie, Annie, are you alright?"

"Please find Peter, please," she begged.

"Annie, you know I will. He can't be far and we'll find him soon. Go with Mr. Barner and take care of those bruises. Sally turned to the man. "I have a few more places to look for Peter. I'll be back as soon as I can."

Sally went directly to Grandma's next door neighbor. By now the owners were standing outside. As Sally approached, the woman asked, "Is that young woman alright?"

Before Sally could answer the man said, "That guy should be put in jail, treating anyone, especially a woman like that. He's pure garbage."

Sally, anxious to ask about Peter, broke in, "Mrs. Wilson's son, Annie's son, Peter…he's five years old and is missing. By any chance have either of you seen him?" The woman looked at her husband and they were silent for what seemed forever, almost like they didn't want to answer.

Finally the man said, "I don't know if this is the boy you're looking for but we've seen a little guy in the woods behind the house next door. I haven't seen him today as the missus and I have been out and just got home a half hour ago."

"Where in the woods?"

"Do you see that big pecan tree?" He pointed. "Well, actually you should ask next door because we've seen her out there too."

"Seen who out there?"

"The woman, the woman next door."

"She's been out there with the little boy?

"Yes, several times. Maybe she can help you."

Sally could hardly believe her ears. It seemed incredible. This woman who wouldn't talk to anybody was playing with children? Sally couldn't imagine it. All of a sudden she was angry. After thanking the couple she went to Grandma's front door, knocked and rang the bell at the same time. No answer. She knocked again, this time louder. Still, no answer. With adrenaline racing through her body she walked quickly to Grandma's back yard and into the woods calling, "Peter...Peter." She came across the huge pecan tree and as she walked around it, she saw a manicured grassy area, certainly foreign to the woods and there was Peter sitting on a large fallen branch. He was crying. Sally ran to him, sat with him, putting her arm around his shoulders. She pulled him close to her body. They sat silently for a couple of minutes. Then Sally heard a noise, like the crackle of dry leaves. At first she thought it was an animal prancing about, but she soon realized the crackling had a rhythm, like footsteps. She looked around but saw nothing.

"Peter was anyone with you here in the woods?" It took a few seconds before he looked at her and slowly shook his head. "You came back here all by yourself?" This time he looked at the ground before nodding that he had. Sally knew this was not the time to ask more questions. She had to bring Peter to Annie. "Peter, let's go. Your Mommy will be so happy to see you." She took his hand and the two walked across the street.

Mrs. Barner saw them crossing the street. "Annie," she called, "I think your friend found your little boy." The door opened and Annie flew towards Peter, snatching him up

in her arms. She didn't let go for a
long, long time.

CHAPTER SEVEN

Sally was dragging the next day after a restless night. She had a hard time falling asleep, thinking about Peter, Annie and Grandma. She couldn't get them out of her mind. Her heart ached for little Peter, seeing him so frightened. Had he seen his father hit his Mom? Sally wondered what affect that would have on a five-year-old child. Then seeing Annie bruised and broken. It was unbelievable to Sally that anyone could be treated so badly. After yesterday she was positive of the past abuses Annie endured. Why does Annie stay with Sam, she wondered. What Sally really had difficulty understanding though, was Grandma and what her relationship was with Peter and why? That question kept rolling over in her mind and she couldn't fathom a reasonable explanation.

The days passed, but Sally found herself still thinking of the happenings of the past week. Rose made matters worse. She'd been taking care of the children while Sally was looking for Peter, so she wanted detailed information. Rose had talked to some neighbors but knew Sally was there so every day she had another question. Sally tried to be civil but it was difficult and there were times she knew she was rude.

Sally stood looking out her back window, watching Tommy play and Jenny pulling herself up in the playpen, throwing her toys out. Tommy scolded her, then picked up her toys and put them back in the playpen. Sally wore a broad smile when the doorbell rang.

When she answered the door she was surprised to see Annie and Peter. She hadn't seen them since Peter went missing.

"Come in, come in, it's good to see you. You've been on my mind all week."

"Sally, I came to say goodbye," Annie said sadly as they went inside.

"Oh, no." Sally was noticeably surprised. "Why?"

Before Annie could answer, Sally asked Peter if he'd like to play with Tommy in the back yard. Peter nodded. Coincidentally, a few weeks prior to the episode with Peter, Sally had her back yard fenced in with a gate latch on the outside and placed too high for little ones to reach. Seeing the boys were playing happily, Sally went back to the living room and again asked Annie, "Why?"

"Peter and I are going to live with my parents. Sally, I don't have to tell you, I'm sure you have seen how abusive Sam is. After last week, I can't put Peter or myself through that kind of living any longer. It isn't living. I've wanted to leave Sam for a long time but didn't have the strength or courage to do so."

"Oh, Annie, I understand. Will Sam stay here?'

"I haven't seen Sam since that horrible day until yesterday. He was unusually calm when I told him I was leaving. He didn't argue but pleaded for me to stay. It was the same old story except this time there's no turning back. When I get settled I'll file for divorce and try to make a new life for Peter and me. I've written down my parents' address and phone number," Annie said handing Sally a piece of paper, then continued "I know your address but please give me your phone number."

Sally scribbled it down and Annie stuck the paper in her pocket. She wanted to ask if Annie talked to Peter about going into the woods behind Grandma's house, but decided this wasn't the time. Instead she said, "The main thing is you are moving on. Just be happy, and please keep in touch." Shortly after tear-filled goodbyes a car pulled up to Annie's house and drove off with Annie, Peter and a few suitcases. "Goodbye friends, God bless and help you both," Sally said to herself as she watched the car disappear.

Sally struggled through the rest of the day, her mind going in seven different directions. Thinking of Tom and wondering when he would be coming home; she worried about Annie and Peter, and of course, her own children. She also wondered where Grandma fit into the picture and felt sure she did somehow. Would Peter say something to Annie about Grandma and being in the woods? Peter is only five and five-year-olds don't know what a secret is, let alone about keeping it. Nothing seemed to make any sense. Sally was deep in thought when the phone's ringing startled her. As she ran to pick it up she said "Oh please God let it be Tom."

"Sally, Sally how are you?"

"Dad, is that you?"

"Yes, honey. How are you and the children?"

"We're just fine. I can't believe I'm talking to you, I miss you so much."

"I miss you too, Sally and that's why I'm calling. Your old Dad wants to come for a visit."

"Oh, that would be wonderful. When can you come?" Sally was excited.

"I was thinking over the Christmas holidays. Being that Tom can't be with you, I figure there's no sense both of us being lonely. How does that sound?"

"That would be great. You make your plans and come as soon as you can. I can't wait to see you." Father and daughter chatted for a few minutes before hanging up. Sally could hardly believe what she just heard. Her Dad didn't like to travel, particularly after her Mom's death two years before. Both her parents had been outgoing with many friends and always on the go. But after her Mom died it all changed. Her Dad had to be pushed to do anything.

Sally was already making plans in her head of all the things they could do together. How wonderful, she thought. Her dad would finally meet Jenny, and Tommy would be thrilled to have a man around the house. It would be absolutely perfect, if only Tom could be with them too. She stood staring at the telephone, willing it to ring again, hoping to hear Tom's voice on the other end.

That evening, after doing a few chores Sally turned out the downstairs lights. Just before going upstairs she looked out the front window. She found herself doing this almost every night to check Grandma's back window. Since the Peter incident, Sally saw only the shadow of one person, not the two she previously had seen. Again this time there was only one. She checked the children, took a shower and readied for bed. She hadn't settled under the covers for long when the phone rang.

"Hello, hello, Tom."

"Is this Mrs. Lester?"

"What" Yes, yes. Who is this?"

"I'm State Trooper McCarthy and there's been an accident."

CHAPTER EIGHT

After a sleepless night, Sally's first thought the next morning was to get to the hospital to make sure Annie and Peter were alright. First, she had to ask Rose to watch her children. Sally knew this would mean a detailed explanation. Although Rose annoyed Sally at times, she felt confident and at ease when the children were in her care, plus the children loved her. Sally dressed and fed the kids, then called Rose. She was shocked to hear the news of the accident, but gladly said she would take care of the children. Sally was able to delay telling Rose the details by promising to tell her everything when she returned home.

As Sally drove to Riverside Hospital she couldn't imagine what to expect. She knew the state trooper got her phone number from the piece of paper Annie put in her pocket.

However, she wasn't Annie's relative so the trooper couldn't give her any information other than two occupants had been taken to Riverside Hospital. Sally told the trooper how Annie and she exchanged phone numbers. She also said she had Annie's parents' number, which she immediately read to him.

Sally trembled as she approached the nurse's station. "Could you please tell me the room number of Mrs. Wilson, Annie Wilson?

The nurse hesitated but finally asked, "Are you a relative?"

"No, I'm just a friend."

"I don't have that information here. Perhaps you could talk to Mrs. Wilson's parents. I believe they are in the surgery waiting room."

'Where is that?"

"Take the elevator to the second floor. Turn right after you get off."

Sally could feel her heart beating in her chest as she entered the room.

She realized she didn't even know Annie's parents' names, let alone what they looked like. She went to the volunteer desk and asked, "Are Mrs.Wilson's parents here?" The volunteer looked at her list. Then pointed to an elderly couple sitting in the far corner. Sally looked at the two older people huddled together holding hands and staring at the floor.

She slowly approached them and said, "I beg your pardon, I'm Sally Lester. I'm a friend of Annie. I live a few doors down from her on Turner Street. Is she alright? Is she in surgery?" Her words were like a freight train. The two raised their sad eyes and looked up, not saying a word, they just looked. It was almost like they didn't even see her.

Kneeling down, Sally put her hands on theirs, hesitating to ask about Annie, almost afraid. It seemed like minutes passed before Annie's

Dad said, "Annie died this morning. Peter is in surgery now."

"Oh, dear God." Gasping to catch her breath Sally managed to tell them how sorry she was before tears streamed down her face. She literally ached watching these two; the woman suffering unspeakable grief and the man trying to be strong for his wife. It was a sad scene to witness. They sat in silence for what seemed a long time. When they did speak their conversation was meager.

Sally asked, "Have you heard the condition of the driver?"

"I understand he isn't in serious condition but I don't know anything else," Mr. Jeffers said. Finally a doctor approached and Mr. Jeffers struggled to stand, probably wanting to shield his wife from whatever the doctor had to tell them.

The doctor put his arm on Mr. Jeffers shoulder as if to reassure him Peter was going to be fine. "We managed to stop the internal bleeding and set his broken bones. He'll be in recovery for some time before going to the pediatric unit. He'll stay in the hospital for about a week for observation. We have to make sure he is stable enough to go home."The doctor suggested they get a bite to eat as it would be awhile before Peter could go to his room.

Sally left the hospital shortly thereafter, needing to get back to her own children. She said goodbye to the Jeffers and asked if she might call to find out the funeral arrangements and also wanted to be informed of Peter's recovery.

Once on Turner Street she immediately went to Rose's house to pick up the children. As soon as she saw Tommy and Jenny she gathered them in her arms and hugged them extra hard, so thankful to have them safe and sound. She thanked Rose for taking care of them and started to leave, but Rose wanted to hear all about Sally's trip.

"Rose, right now I have to go home, it's been a long trying day and I am so tired."

"I understand..." but Sally knew she didn't. When she asked Rose to mind the children she told her about the accident and that Annie and Peter were taken to the hospital. Knowing Rose, Sally knew she wanted all the details and she wouldn't be satisfied until she did.

"Rose...Annie was killed in the accident."

"No, no! How horrible," she screamed, "and that poor little boy?"

"Peter will be fine in time. He has a few broken bones."

"How did it happen?"

"I haven't the answers. Annie's parents were so distraught it would have been unkind to ask a lot of questions."

"This is terrible, that poor child."

"Yes, it is."

By this time Rose was near hysterics and Jenny started to cry, so Sally was finally able to leave. She just got in her front door and heard the phone ringing. With Jenny still in her arms she picked up the receiver.

"Do you know where my wife is?" Sally recognized Sam's voice.

CHAPTER NINE

With Thanksgiving over, Christmas was right around the corner. Sally's Dad was due to arrive in a week. Sally was excited, and really needed someone to lean on. The past couple of weeks had many difficult days and without Tom they were even more so.

A few days before her Dad arrived Sally took her kids to see Peter at his grandparents. Peter was doing well and it meant so much to the Jeffers to have him there. Peter still had a cast on his leg which Tommy thought was cool and had fun scribbling on it. Before they left, the Jeffers mentioned Sam was going to court to get permanent custody of Peter, which of course they were determined to fight.

At that point Sally told the Jeffers about the phone call from Sam just after she returned from the hospital. "I was upset and really didn't know what to say to him but I did tell him I thought he should get in touch with you."

"Did you hear from him?"

"Not then. The only contact we've had was his call concerning custody of Peter. Did you tell him Annie was killed in the accident?"

"He was becoming belligerent and started yelling. After I told him to call you he accused me of lying, saying, "She's not there." I was beginning to think he had no idea there had even been an accident. I guess he thought I meant Annie was at your house. I then said "I'm sorry Sam, Annie's gone." He cursed and said he knew she wasn't on Turner Street and demanded I tell him where she was. I was so upset by then, I told him I didn't know and hung up the phone. I prayed he wouldn't call back. He didn't."

"I'm so sorry he put you through that. He's not a nice person," Mrs. Jeffers said.

"No, he's not. For several days I kept an eye on their house and was glad there was no sign of Sam. I was relieved but not long after his truck roared down the street. Even his presence upset me."

"Is Sam living there now?" Mr. Jeffers asked.

"No, he filled up his truck with furniture and stuff from the house and left. Several days later a man drove up to the house and planted a FOR SALE sign in the front yard."

"Good, then you won't be bothered with him and that's good news."

"I agree and it's probably a relief to all on Turner Street, most of all me."

They chatted awhile longer, then Sally left for home. She was glad to see Peter so happy although she hoped she hadn't upset the Jeffers talking about Sam. The whole situation would make anybody miserable.

It was a balmy afternoon the next day and Sally took advantage of it by taking a walk with the children. She noticed many of her neighbors were also enjoying the weather and sitting on their porches. They waved to Sally and some even came down to see the kids and to chat a bit. When she passed Annie's house the FOR SALE sign was still there. She continued to walk to the end of the street then crossed over to the other side.

Grandma too, was rocking on her front porch. As Sally approached, she waved and said, "Good Afternoon." The old woman stood and Sally sighed knowing she would go into the house and close her door.

However, to Sally's amazement, Grandma descended her porch stairs and said, "Missy, have you seen Peter?"

"Why yes, just the other day."

"Where, at his grandparents?"

"Yes."

"Is he alright?"

"Oh, yes."

"Is he still in a cast?"

"I believe it's to be taken off soon."

"Are you sure?"

"That's what his grandparents told me."

With that Grandma, not saying another word, she turned and went up the stairs and into her house. Sally stood there watching her disappear, before continuing their walk. She was really disturbed and couldn't help wondering, how in the world does that woman know about Peter, the accident, where he is now and she even knows about his cast. How does she know all of this? She never goes anywhere, doesn't have mail delivered and from all accounts doesn't see anyone. But how can I forget about that second shadow in the back window I see now and again late at night? Come to think of it there have been shadows lately. Who is coming late at night and is that person her contact with the outside world? There are so many questions and so few answers. No wonder most people here think Grandma is one crazy lady.

Back at her house Sally brought the kids to the back yard where they could play. She sat in a lawn chair enjoying them. Jenny crawled in the grass, examining it carefully while Tommy buzzed her with his toy plane. Each time he buzzed her, Jenny giggled. Sally realized this was the joy of her life. She ran into the house and got her camera to take pictures of the two kids playing and laughing. She knew Tom would get a kick out of seeing the pictures.

After lunch, Sally settled the children upstairs for their naps. She got pen and paper and went out on the porch to write to Tom. She told him how excited she was her Dad would be arriving soon. Sally also wrote about her latest encounter with Grandma, but most of all, how wonderful it would be when he's home. She wouldn't be so preoccupied with Grandma and the happenings on Turner Street then.

Or would she?

CHAPTER TEN

Finally, the day arrived for Sally's Dad to visit. Patiently waiting on her front porch, she thought about how long it had been since she had seen her father. The two years had flown by with Tom starting his job at the insurance company and going to school a couple of nights a week. Tommy was in the terrible two's which kept Sally on the go. Then too, making matters more difficult Sally had miscarried a little girl. Her Dad was so lost after the death of her Mother he made no attempt to do anything or see anyone. His last phone call telling her he wanted to come was unexpected, but Sally was thrilled and couldn't wait to see him. She had always kept in touch with her Dad and one of her last calls mentioned how lonely the coming holiday season would be with Tom overseas. She thought that's what prompted his visit now. Neither would be lonely. How wonderful.

The car pulled into the driveway and Sally jumped to her feet. She practically flew down the steps and into the arms of her Dad. After many hugs and kisses they got his luggage from the car. Two suitcases, one with her Dad's belongings, the other filled with goodies for his grandchildren.

Once in the house, father and daughter had a chance to be together while the children were still napping. They had two years to get caught up on and found much to talk about.

And it didn't take long for Sally's Dad, to become the center of attraction for all in the Lester's lives and Grandpa couldn't get enough of Jenny and Tommy. They were either sitting on his lap or he was on the floor playing with them. Sally was the happiest she'd been in a long time.

Rose Trundale couldn't wait another minute. She knocked on the front door, opened it and called, "Yoo-hoo, Sally, it's Rose."

Of course she was already in the door and Sally knew her curiosity had gotten the best of her. "Come in Rose," Sally called.

"I hope I'm not bothering you."

"Come in the kitchen. I want you to meet my Dad."

"I'd love to."

"Rose, this is my father, Joe Carter." After the formalities, they sat around the kitchen table and chatted. Rose was in her glory.

Joe Carter enjoyed taking the kids for walks, which also gave him a chance to meet some of the neighbors. Sally was equally happy to see her father returning to the warm friendly guy he truly was.

On one such walk he noticed the woman down the block who was not very amicable. He smiled, waved and said good day. Of course that woman was Grandma. That night Sally told her Dad about the woman everyone called Grandma and all her idiosyncrasies. "She really is strange, Dad."

"So it sounds."

"You can imagine how amazed I was when last week we actually had a conversation."

"What was that about?"

"She wanted to know about the little boy, Peter, who was injured in the horrific accident I told you about."

"How did she know about Peter?"

"I don't know but she certainly knew all about him."

"Hmm, strange."

"Talking about Peter, I'd like you to meet him and his grandparents. Maybe we could bring Peter here for a play day with Tommy."

"Sure, let's do it."

A phone call was made. Plans to pick up Peter the next day for a play day and sleepover were finalized.

Sally invited Peter's grandparents for dinner the following evening and then Peter could go home with them. Before Mrs. Jeffers agreed to this arrangement she had to be assured that Sam was nowhere around Turner Street.

"I haven't seen any sign of him since he loaded his truck with things from the house," Sally told her.

The next morning Sally, Grandpa and the kids drove the ten miles to get Peter. They were warmly greeted by the Jeffers and got a huge smile from Peter. Although still quiet, Peter's whole being seemed so much more relaxed and that beautiful smile more frequent. His cast was off and he was walking well. On the drive back to Turner Street there was much chatter between the two boys. Even Jenny chimed in with her baby language. She missed Peter too.

Having both Grandpa and Peter at his house, Tommy was in his glory.

The boys had a great time during the day and when they got in bed that night there was much giggling, although it didn't last long before they were sound asleep. It was a day to remember. Sally got her call from Tom and her Dad was able to speak to him too. Sally thought everything was wonderful. But why do things always have to change?

CHAPTER ELEVEN

Everyone was up bright early so after breakfast the boys and Grandpa went out back to play ball. After a while Peter said, "Let's go play in the woods."

"Where are the woods?" Grandpa asked.

"Down there, down the block," Peter pointed in the direction of Grandma's house, "See behind that house?"

"What do you say about that, Tommy?"

"Yeah, let's go." Tommy was already at the gate waiting for Grandpa to unlock it.

"Do you guys play there often?" Tommy shook his head but Peter just shrugged. Grandpa yelled in the back door, "Sally, the boys and I are going for a walk."

"Have fun," Sally called back.

Off they went, Peter more or less leading the way. When they were close to Grandma's house, Peter walked to her back yard. Sally's Dad was hesitant, having heard about this woman and asked Peter if he played there before. Peter didn't answer but kept going. They entered the woods and it wasn't long before they were at the pecan tree. Joe Carter was amazed to see this small well-kept parcel of land amidst the dense woods. At the same time he noticed a marked change in Peter. He was very quiet, almost tense. On the other hand, Tommy ran all over the place picking up fallen pecans. They hadn't been there but a few minutes when Grandma appeared. She walked directly to Joe Carter and asked, "What are you doing? You have no business being here, this is private property."

"I'm sorry, I wasn't aware this was private property. The boys,

Peter…" He didn't finish what he wanted to say, thinking better of it. "Come on boys, time to go. Come, come."

Tommy took his Grandfather's hand right away. Peter walked slowly towards them. Joe Carter looked back and called Peter again. He noticed Grandma smiling at Peter, and Peter looked wide-eyed at her. When they were almost to the edge of the woods, Mr. Carter turned again to tell Peter to hurry and catch up. At that moment Grandma bent down saying something in Peter's ear.

"Peter we have to go now. Hurry along."

This time Peter ran and caught up with Tommy and Mr. Carter. The rest of the way back Peter was quiet. He actually seemed to be preoccupied. Joe Carter just couldn't put his finger on Peter's demeanor. When they reached their house, Grandpa left the boys to play in the yard and went inside. Sally and Jenny were playing in the living room. Sally called, "Dad is that you?"

"Yeah, honey."

"That was a quick walk," she said entering the kitchen.

Joe Carter stood by the window looking out at the boys. Tommy was trying to get Peter to play catch but Peter just stood there. It seemed he didn't want to play anything.

"Was it a good walk?"

Her Dad turned from the window with a puzzled look.

"Dad, what's the matter? Did the boys misbehave?"

"No, no." He told her about what happened in the woods.

"You know Dad that woman has some kind of hold on Peter but I can't figure out what."

"I agree. Peter's whole bearing changed once he saw her. He's still in a state. Look at him just standing there."

As the day went on Peter gradually was more himself and by the time his grandparents arrived he was fine. They had a pleasant time together and when dinner was over the boys went to the living room to play games. When they were out of earshot, Sally asked the Jeffers if they heard anything more about the custody case.

"Nothing definite yet but we called the court. We found out Mr. Wilson requested a hearing in family court. We asked to have it scheduled as soon as possible. Whether that means anything, who knows? We thought there's no harm in asking," Mrs. Jeffers told them.

"I'm sure you're both anxious to get this settled once and for all," Sally remarked.

"Yes, I'm fearful Sam will snatch Peter from us. We keep a sharp eye on him all the time. It's difficult on us as well as Peter. I'm sure he wonders why we're always watching him." They talked awhile and before leaving told Sally how much they enjoyed the evening. "Peter always has a great time with Tommy."

As they said their goodbyes they promised to keep in touch. When they heard anything further concerning the hearing they'd immediately call. Tommy wasn't happy to see Peter leave but the Jeffers promised they could play together again soon.

When the kitchen was cleaned up and the children tucked in bed, Sally and her Dad went outside. They discussed the day's events as well as their time together. "What a lovely evening Sally. I enjoyed meeting the Jeffers. They are special people and Peter is a lucky boy. Plus Sally, your dinner was delicious." Joe complimented his daughter.

"I think you may be just a little prejudice."

"No, I mean it and the Jeffers certainly enjoyed it too." They sat quietly until her dad broke the silence and said, "You know, Sally I just can't get that little boy out of my mind."

"You mean Peter?"

"Yes, I guess what bothers me the most is the power that woman seems to hold over him."

"Yeah, the problem is Peter won't talk about her to anyone."

They sat there discussing the problem but didn't come to any conclusion about Grandma's hold over Peter. Finally Joe said, "Well, my dear tomorrow is a busy day so I guess we should call it a night. We're not going to solve anything, at least not tonight."

"You're right. The days before Christmas are always hectic," Sally said as the two started for the front door. "Dad, Dad look, look at the

back window of Grandma's house.
See the two shadows?"

CHAPTER TWELVE

With Christmas Eve in a day, there was much hustle and bustle in the Lester household. For that matter, there was hustle and bustle in the whole neighborhood. Some houses were decorated, lights trimming their porches and brightly lit trees could be seen through the windows. Although Tommy was waiting as patiently as a four-year-old could, it was decided to put the tree up Christmas Eve with Grandpa in charge. Joe Carter had bought so many decorations he could decorate the entire neighborhood. It was duly noted by neighbor Rose, to all who would listen, that Grandma's house hadn't changed one bit for the holidays, followed by, "that woman has no heart."

Sally baked Christmas cookies during the week and shared them with Tommy's friends and neighbors. One evening she even put some in a container on Grandma's porch. Joe Carter thought it was unnecessary, "Sally, why do you bother? You know she doesn't share the Christmas Spirit."

"I know Dad, but I really feel for her."

"Why? Her attitude is of her own making."

"Yes, I know that too, but no one bothers their head about her."

"Probably the reason is she doesn't bother with anyone herself."

"It's too bad. She obviously is an unhappy person."

"We don't know that either. Maybe we're reading a lot into her actions."

"How can you say that, Dad?"

"Think about it. What do we really know about her? We presume, but we don't know." Joe put his arm around his daughter. "Sally I do admire you, do continue to be an angel of mercy."

However, Sally was disheartened the next morning to find the cookies back on her front porch. So much for being an angel of mercy, Sally smiled to herself. Walking into the kitchen she announced, "Dad you were right. The cookies are back."

"You tried honey, that's all you can do."

"Maybe, but think about it, how did she know they came from us and who delivered them here?"

"Well, we do know there's another person there at night and most likely he returned it."

"What makes you think it's a he?"

"I don't know, the head of the second shadow we see doesn't appear to have much hair. It's really just a guess."

There was no time to try and figure out Grandma. Christmas Eve morning arrived along with a hundred and one things to do readying for the holiday. Sally and her Dad were busy all day, at times complicated by Tommy's excitement that grew by the minute. Jenny sat in her jumper seat happily taking it all in. Finally, after the children were settled in bed for the night, Sally wrapped presents while Grandpa did an outstanding job of decorating the tree. While they were busy, Rose popped in, laden with gifts.

"My heavens Rose, what is all this?" Sally couldn't get over her armful of gifts.

"Don't be silly. Your children are special and I wanted them to know Santa Claus left presents for them at my house too. I don't have any little ones to buy for and it gave me such pleasure to buy for Tommy and Jenny."

"Rose, how sweet and thank you so much." Sally said, thinking how glad she had bought a gift for Rose from the children.

"What are your plans tomorrow?" Joe asked Rose.

"I really don't have any definite plans."

Sally gave Rose a hug and said, "Yes, you do, Rose. We'd love to have you join us for dinner tomorrow around four."

It was obvious Rose was taken aback, "I'd love to. It will be a Merry Christmas after all, especially being with my dear friends. Thank you. I'll be going now. I know you two have a lot to do."

Sally walked Rose to the door and when she came back in the living room her Dad gave her a big hug and said, "Isn't it great to do the right thing? Merry Christmas, Sal. You not only gave Rose one but certainly you've given me one also. I love you, honey." They hugged, then Joe said, "We better get a move on and finish here." It was ten forty-five before the two finally sat down. Although tired, they admired the tree and all the packages underneath.

"Dad, the tree looks beautiful with so many presents under the tree for the children. Too many I..." Before she could finish, the doorbell rang. "Who in the world could that be at this time of night?" Sally asked.

Joe smiled, "Maybe some carolers. Go see."

She opened the door. "Oh, my God," she cried and was quickly enveloped in the arms of Tom. It took some time for Sally to come down to earth with the reality that her beloved husband was actually home. He explained his tour had been extended so they gave him a ten-day leave. Although he'd told Grandpa on the phone, he wanted to surprise Sally. And surprised she was. Shortly after Tom's arrival, Joe excused himself, knowing this wasn't the place for a father. As he ascended the stairs he couldn't help but notice the love between his daughter and Tom. The couple talked for a few minutes, before Sally took Tom by the hand upstairs to the children's room. With his arm tightly around Sally he looked down at his son. "Sweetheart, he's grown so much."

"Yes, and he's such a nice boy. A real boy, but he's sweet at the same time. You'll see."

"I can't wait. And now our baby girl Jenny," he said as they moved toward the crib. Tom stood staring at his daughter, seeing her for the first time. Tears of joy rolled down his cheeks, "She's so beautiful," he whispered. "She's going to look like her pretty mommy." He stood there for a couple of minutes before together they tiptoed out of the room. Tom closed the door and took Sally in his arms, "I'm so sorry I wasn't there for you, darling but never again. I have six more months then I'll be home for good."

"I can't believe you're here now. Six months will be an eternity."

"I've missed you beyond words. I want to be here with you enjoying our children." They kissed passionately and went back downstairs to lock up and turn out lights. Everything was secured for the night except for the tree lights. The couple stood there arm in arm.

"Pinch me," said Sally.

"Gladly."

"Oh Tom," she laughed "I just want to be sure I'm not dreaming." He squeezed her tightly and with that the two went up to their bedroom where they lay in each other's arms and became one as they made love.

CHAPTER THIRTEEN

The holiday season in the Lester home was a happy time for all. It didn't take long for Tommy to reconnect with his Dad. Grandpa, Daddy and son had fun playing in the yard with Jenny in her swing on the sidelines, watching with glee. During the entire time Sally had a smile on her face. She couldn't have been happier.

Tom was also able to have a long talk with his father-in-law, most of all thanking him. "Joe, I can't thank you enough for being here for Sally and the kids. It's made my being away from home a little easier."

"The thanks is for you and Sally. Being here has made me come alive again. I was becoming a lonely, grouchy old man."

"Lonely, maybe, grouchy, no."

"Well, it's been a joy to be here and your children have given me a new lease on life."

"I'll be discharged shortly after I get back. Sally and I have talked and we both want to locate near you."

"You get back safely and then we'll talk. Although, you know I think that's the most brilliant idea you two have come up with."

Tom laughed, "You really think so?"

"You bet. I have to be back home by the end of month. I hadn't planned on staying this long. Even though it's been one of the best times of my life, I do have things I must attend to. But I assure you I'll be in constant touch with Sally and the kids."

Tom got up and gave Joe a hug. "Thanks."

Sally invited Peter and his grandparents for lunch so the kids could play together and to meet Tom. It was so good to see them. Peter seemed happier than Sally had ever seen him.

When lunch was over the kids went out to play with their new toys. The adults sat around the table enjoying a cup of tea and homemade cookies. Sally had a feeling Mrs. Jeffers wanted to talk to them. Indeed, she did, "We got a letter from Sam's attorney. There will be a custody hearing in family court."

"Oh, no," Sally gasped, "I didn't think he'd really go through with it. I can't imagine why, he never bothered much when he did have him. You took care of Peter Monday through Friday and he was on Turner Street only on the weekends."

"Yes, I mentioned that to him when he first stopped by. And by the way, that's the only time we've seen him. He said that wasn't his idea, it was Annie who insisted."

"I would think she had a good reason."

"I wonder if you, Sally or anyone else on Turner Street would be willing to testify against Sam on Peter's behalf? I have no idea what went on here but I do know Peter arrived at our house very sad on Mondays. I guess a better word would be upset."

"Did Annie ever mention anything to you about Sam?"

"No, probably because she knew we never wanted her to marry Sam, so there were very few conversations about him. Being her mother though, we knew she wasn't happy." They sat at the table trying to figure out who might have pertinent information and be willing to testify.

"Maybe Annie's neighbor, Mr. Barner could help. He came to her aid when Sam knocked her to the ground," Sally said.

"Right, and there's Grandma's next door neighbor. They actually saw Peter go into the woods and Grandma being there with him. She might have some input." Joe wondered out loud.

As soon as Grandma's name was mentioned it was like a light bulb went on. "Grandma," Joe Carter said, "Of course, Grandma is the one to testify. She knows more about Peter than anyone."

Sally told the Jeffers the entire story about Grandma and Peter going into the woods behind her house. She also mentioned how Peter would never say why he was there. At the same time though, he really seemed to like Grandma very much. Joe Carter added just how strange Grandma was. They sat there trying to figure out the best approach to convince Grandma to testify. They couldn't get a court order because they didn't even know the woman's name.

Finally Joe said, "There's only one way to solve this and that's if we go directly to her and ask."

"Dad, you know she won't even answer the door, let alone talk to anyone."

"That's probably true but what about that second shadow? We know someone else is there, at least some nights."

Joe thought for a moment, then directing his words to the Jeffers said, "I will go myself and try to speak to Grandma. If I can't, I will speak to whomever is in her house at night. I truly think that's our answer."

"I agree, Dad, although I'm not sure we'll get the results we need."

"Maybe not, but we have to try. In the meantime, Sally you talk to the neighbors and see if they know something that might help."

"Mr. Carter, I can't thank you enough." Mr. Jeffers said.

"It might take a while because whoever it is, doesn't appear to be there every night," Joe explained.

Right after the New Year celebration was over so was Tom's leave. It was harder than ever to say goodbye. Joe said his goodbye then took the little ones out back so Tom and Sally could be alone. Sally, clinging to her husband asked, "Tom, will you have to go back to the middle- east again?"

"I won't know until I report to the base but I'll call you as soon as I know." He looked down at her tearful eyes. "There's a chance I might stay state-side. I sure hope I do but as you know honey, what I want and they want isn't always the same." They held each other closely and kissed long and tenderly. Finally, Tom let her go and got into his rental car. Sally, trying very hard not to break down, kissed him again through the open car window and begged him to be safe. As the car eased down the driveway and out onto Turner Street, Sally watched until he was out of sight.

Sally and her Dad had made it a point to sit on the front porch later in the evening, hoping to see that all important second shadow. The night came about a week after Tom left. On this particular night, about ten o'clock, they saw the two shadows in Grandma's back window.

Joe Carter rushed to the back door of Grandma's house and knocked several times.

CHAPTER FOURTEEN

Sally watched her Dad as he marched towards Grandma's house. She knew how determined he was to speak to Grandma, but Sally herself had doubts. Soon he was out of sight, Sally was pacing on her own front porch.

Joe wasted no time. He went directly to Grandma's back door and knocked. No answer. He knocked again. No answer, but this time he heard voices. He waited a minute and rapped on the door once again. Still, no one opened the door. Joe was determined so he knocked once more. Suddenly, the door opened and there stood a man of about fifty years old. This surprised Joe. In his mind the shadow was that of a young man. This man stood there looking at Joe and finally asked, "What the hell is the matter with you, coming around at this time of night? What the…what's your problem?"

"Sir, my name is Joe Carter. I'm Sally Lester's father. She lives at the end of this street. I came to speak to the woman who lives here."

"Really. What for?"

"It's very important." Joe said a little louder, hoping Grandma was nearby behind the half closed door.

At that point the man closed the door and stepped outside, closing the screen door behind him. He said, "Look, I don't know what you're up to but my aunt doesn't want to speak to you or anyone else."

"Sir."

"My name is George. What the hell is this sir business?"

"George, I can't impress enough how important this is."

"Okay. Impress me."

"Look. If you won't let me see her, can you at least give her a message?"

"That's not impressing me at all."

"George, I'm not here to impress anyone. I'm here because I have something important to talk about with your aunt. Only she can help in this matter."

"You think so?"

"I know so. Will you give her a message?"

"Yeah, I guess so."

"Good. Tell her that the little boy Peter…she'll know who that is"…before Joe could finish, George said, "Peter, you say? That's odd."

"Yes, Peter." Then Joe quickly added, "tell her Peter needs her help and we can't delay. Time is of the essence."

"What do you mean, help? I don't know what's going on here."

"Please George, just give her that message. I'll come back tomorrow night at eight-thirty to speak to her."

"That'll be the day."

"Please, George."

"Okay. Okay, what did you say your name was?"

"Joe. Joe Carter."

"Don't misunderstand me. I know what the people in the neighborhood think of my aunt. She has every right to do and act the way she wants. People shouldn't judge her. I'll tell her. I don't know if I'll be back tomorrow. Most likely my son might be."

I'd appreciate it. By the way, I respect your aunt's wishes and I wouldn't intrude if my talking to her wasn't important. Thanks a lot George. I'll be back tomorrow night."

Joe walked quickly home. As soon as Sally caught sight of him she ran down the steps. "Dad, I was worried. What happened?"

"Let's get in the house and I'll tell you."

Once inside they turned off the porch light and sat in the kitchen.

Sally got two cold beers out of the fridge while Joe related exactly what happened. Sally was relieved that her Dad was alright, but said. "I wish I felt differently, but I just don't think she'll talk to you. It's so unlike her. It sounds like George thinks so too."

"I do think George will tell his aunt what I said and hopefully how important it is that I need to speak with her. We'll have to keep our fingers crossed and hope for the best. One thing though, as soon as I mentioned the name Peter, a strange look came over him. George thought that was odd."

"What do you think that was about?"

"I don't know honey, but I think it's about time we called it a night." They gladly did knowing there was nothing more that could be accomplished tonight.

Sally was the first one up the next morning. She prepared her special pancake batter when she heard Jenny cry. She hurried upstairs hoping the baby's cry didn't wake Tommy and Grandpa. It did. Soon the entire family was around the kitchen table happily eating pancakes when Grandpa said, "How about we all go to the park by the river this morning?"

He quickly got an answer from Tommy, "Yeah, I want to go on the big kid swing."

Jenny clapped her sticky pancake hands. She evidently thought going to the park was a good idea, too.

"Okay, Sally you get the kids dressed and I'll clean up the kitchen." He did and got another cup of coffee, then called upstairs, "Grandpa is going to sit on the porch and read the paper while you get dressed."

"Alright, we'll be down shortly."

As Joe opened the door, something fell to the floor. It was an envelope. He tried to maneuver picking it up, not spilling the hot coffee or dropping the paper and keeping his balance. Finally settled in the chair, he looked at the envelope. It was addressed to Mr. Joe Carter. Who in the world could this be from, maybe George? He quickly opened it. No, it wasn't from George, rather it read, "This is from the woman you call Grandma."

CHAPTER FIFTEEN

Joe scanned the short note to see if Grandma wrote her name at the bottom. She didn't. He heard Sally and the kids come downstairs and shoved the note into his pocket. Ever since Christmas and especially after Tom's leave was over, it seemed everything was centered between Grandma and Peter. Joe thought they should have a day, at least part of one, away from Turner Street and its problems. He helped Sally get the children settled in their car seats. Off they went.

"Dad, it's a beautiful day. I'm so glad you suggested going to the park." It was perfect. You could feel everyone's spirit lifted. The morning was filled with laughter and fun. They even went to the hot dog stand for lunch before returning home. Jenny was asleep practically before she was buckled into her car seat and Tommy wasn't far behind. When they got home Grandpa carried Jenny upstairs, still asleep, and put her in her crib. Tommy was so sleepy he barely made it up the stairs.

With the children tucked in, Sally and Joe went to the kitchen for a nice cold glass of ice tea. "That was a really a fun morning, Dad. We probably should consider taking a nap ourselves. Tommy had you running all over the park."

"True, and these old legs feel it. I think a nap is probably a good idea."

"You better take one before the children are ready for a second round."

"Yes, but first I have to call the car rental place and make arrangements to go to the airport, then I have something to show you."

"Dad, I just hate to think about you leaving."

"Believe me honey, I feel the same way, but I have to get home to take care of business." Sally told him many times she would drive him to the airport, but he wouldn't hear of it. She got the phone number and Joe made the necessary arrangements.

"What is it you wanted to show me Dad?"

"This morning I went out to read the paper, and as I opened the door this fell to the floor," Joe said as he reached into his pocket, took out the envelope and handed it to Sally.

"What is it Dad?"

"It's a note. Are you ready for this?"

"A note? Who from?"

"Grandma."

"Grandma?" Sally gasped

"Yes, read it." Sally took the note and read it out loud.

This is from the woman you all call Grandma.

I do not want to talk to you about little Peter

now or at any time. Peter is a sweet little boy

and I'm glad he is in the good hands of his grand-

parents. I don't have anything further to say.

Sally stared at the paper for a minute, "I guess that's that. I'm surprised she even bothered to write the note."

"I don't know honey, as you said her writing the note surprised you. You thought that was so unlike her."

"Yes, but she made it clear she isn't going to talk to anyone," Sally said waving the note in front of her Dad.

"That may be so, but I feel for her to do something so unlike her, there might be more."

"More what?"

"I don't know. It's just a feeling."

"Oh Dad, I think we have to give up."

Her Dad took the note from Sally's waving hands, "Not so fast. I'll play her game and write a note back."

"What will you write?"

"I'll tell her exactly what the situation is. Why Peter needs her help. Why it's important for her to testify in family court to prevent Sam from getting full custody of Peter. Do you have note paper handy, Sal?" She nodded, as she went to get paper and pen. While Joe was composing his note, the phone rang. Sally answered. She talked on the phone while her Dad continued to write. He wrote what he said he would. It was short and to the point.

"Well, Dad a miracle is going to have to happen very soon."

"Why's that?" Joe asked.

"That was Peter's grandmother on the phone."

"And?"

"And the court date is in two weeks."

Joe stared into space for a moment. "Two weeks, huh?" Sally nodded "That would be a couple of days before my flight home." Neither said anything realizing they really had nothing substantial to help the Jeffers. Finally Joe asked, "You talked to Mr. Barner, right?"

"Yes, and he will testify. The next door neighbors are very hesitant. I rather doubt they'll testify. I couldn't get a definite answer, but I'll try again."

"Good. No one else on Turner Street had anything to contribute?"

"No. Everyone I talked with said they saw very little of Peter so couldn't be of any help."

"Good enough. Now I just need an envelope. Sally fetched him one which he sealed and wrote in quotes on the front, "Grandma."

As he started down the front steps, Sally asked, "You're not going to deliver that in broad daylight are you?" He didn't answer but continued on his way. He went up the steps to Grandma's front porch, rang the doorbell and tucked the envelope between the screen and front doors. No one answered, which didn't surprise Joe. He didn't bother to wait but started back to the Lester house.

Someone did answer the door though, bent down, picked up the envelope and closed the door again. Joe was barely out of sight.

CHAPTER SIXTEEN

The thought of the court date just a few days away, and her father leaving shortly thereafter put Sally in a blue funk. She made arrangements with Rose, to care for the children while she was at court. Of course, Rose was miffed that she wasn't involved in any of the court proceedings. Sally was sure there wasn't anyone on Turner Street that Rose hadn't made aware of the goings on.

Sally spoke with the Jeffers' lawyer concerning her testimony and the questions she would be asked, which made her all the more nervous about testifying.

Her Dad tried to keep everything light and upbeat, but at times couldn't hide his concerns. He was disappointed that he failed to get Grandma to testify. He still was convinced that her testimony would clinch the judge's decision in favor of the Jeffers. Joe never received a reply from his note to Grandma, and her rear window where they had seen shadows now was covered with dark shades, eliminating their capability of knowing if Grandma had night time visitors.

Sally and her Dad sat at the kitchen table sipping a second cup of coffee. As much as they tried to talk about anything other than going to court, invariably the conversation wound up there. "I'll sure be glad when tomorrow comes and goes," Sally said.

"I know honey," her Dad said understanding his daughter's anxiety, "but you know you did all you could on Peter's behalf."

"But is it enough?" she questioned.

"Whether it is or not, you did everything possible and no one can do better than that." At that moment

Tommy came barreling through the door to get one of his toys. "Grandpa, come out and play," he yelled on his way out again.

"Honestly, there is nothing like children to get your mind off your problems," Grandpa said as he went out the door to join his grandson.

The day and evening dragged, although they had several visitors at the Lester house. Rose popped in and out making sure she was updated on the very latest. Sally was beginning to think Rose had a crush on her Dad, as well as being nosey. Also, Grandma's next door neighbor stopped by mid-afternoon. Sally recognized her but didn't know her name. "I'm so sorry to come unannounced," the woman said.

"Oh, don't be silly. Come into the living room and meet my father. What was your name again?"

"It's Emily Manning," she replied. With introductions over, Sally asked Emily to sit with them but she said nervously, "No, no I just wanted to tell you my husband and I are sorry we couldn't help you and that little boy." After Sally reassured her she understood, the lady left.

"What was that all about?" Joe asked.

"I have no idea."

Although neither Sally nor her Dad slept well, they were up bright and early the next morning. Joe was anxious to go to court and Sally wished it was over. Rose arrived almost an hour earlier than she was due, making things more hectic, but finally Joe and Sally were on their way to the court house.

The proceedings began on time. The court room was surprisingly full, even though at a hearing in family court only persons concerned with the case were allowed, with no spectators. Sam and his lawyer were surrounded with what appeared to be family and many friends. Peter's grandparents, lawyer and a few of their family members attended, as well as some witnesses from Turner Street. Mr. and Mrs. Jeffers, along with a younger woman were seated with their attorney, directly in front of Sally and Joe. Before the proceedings began, Sally talked to them for a short time and asked Mrs. Jeffers how Peter was. She said he was fine and was in an anteroom in the courthouse. "Is he alright? Does he know what's going on?" Sally questioned.

"He's good and we've given him a general idea as to why he is here. As far as realizing what this hearing is about, I doubt he understands the full consequences of what's happening." She started to say more when a hush came over the room as Children's Court Judge Mathews entered, taking his seat. He rapped his gavel for silence, then sorted papers, adjusting them to his liking. He rested his elbows on the table, folded his hands and slowly looked from right to left of the courtroom, studying the occupants.

Then he said, "We are here today to consider the immediate needs of the child, Peter John Wilson, involved in this case. We will keep the focus on this child's need for permanence and resolution, embracing his safety and health before all else." The judge also reminded the witnesses they had been sworn under oath to tell the truth.

After the formalities of the court hearing were over, testimony began. The lawyers for both parties were selected by the family members involved and came well prepared in child custody hearings. The Petitioner's side was heard first. There were several family members, friends and Sam's employer who testified on his behalf, telling the court of Sam's devotion to his son, Peter and how he longed to be with him now and always. Sam then took the stand and declared his love for his son and Peter's great need to be with his father and not elderly grandparents.

At that point the respondent's lawyer asked Sam one question. "When was the last time you saw your son?"

Sam gulped, "Oh, not that long ago."

"Really? Can you give me a more exact time?"

Sam's head lowered and mumbled a barely audible, "Just before the accident."

"Sir, did I hear you say just before the accident?"

"Yeah, you heard." Sam was getting testy at this point. "What has that got to do with my son?"

"Sir, isn't it true that you hadn't seen your son for several weeks before the accident, therefore you actually haven't seen your son in over two and a half months and have made no attempt to do so?"

"That's crazy. It wasn't several weeks," Sam's voice was agitated.

The attorney asked, emphasizing each word, "Exactly how long before the accident did you see your son?"

"Exactly, I can't remember."

"That will be all," and the attorney sat down.

CHAPTER SEVENTEEN

The judge ordered a ten minute recess for Sam Wilson to compose himself after his tirade during questioning. Sam, no doubt, realized the hearing wasn't going well for his case.

When testimony resumed, Mr. Barner of Turner Street was called. He gave, in detail, his eyewitness account of Sam's brutal attack on Annie, his slapping her so hard she fell to the ground, then leaving her there as he sped off in his truck.

Sally's testimony was equally damning against Sam's character. She told of seeing Annie's bruises on several different occasions and how terrified Annie was of Sam.

Sam's attorney asked, "Did you actually see Mr. Wilson strike his wife on these several occasions?"

"I saw Mr. Wilson hit his wife only once.

"When was that?"

"The day he slapped Annie's face so hard she fell to the sidewalk."

"The other times you assumed Mrs. Wilson's bruises were caused by her husband?"

"Yes, but Annie did tell me she was afraid of her husband. The attorney had no further questions and sat down.

Sally turned to the Judge. "Annie adored her son, Peter. She felt Peter was safe only during the weekdays when he was with her parents who cared for him." It was during her testimony, the court clerk handed the judge a slip of paper.

When Peter's grandmother, Mrs. Jeffers was finally called to the stand, she told how she and Mr. Jeffers took care of Peter every week day from Monday morning until late Friday afternoon. She recounted that when Peter arrived he was withdrawn and quiet but as the week went on, he became one happy little camper, so to speak.

"Mrs. Jeffers, after your daughter Annie's death, did Sam Wilson visit his son Peter while he was living at your house?

"No. Today is the first time we saw him."

"Has Mr. Wilson called your home to talk to his son?"

"No. He did call once and spoke to my husband. Mr. Wilson informed us he was taking us to court for custody of Peter." Mrs. Jeffers then took her seat.

Judge Mathews picked up the note the clerk gave him previously and re-read it. He then called for a fifteen minute break. Most everyone went out in the hallway to stretch. Joe and Sally, as well as the Jeffers thought the testimony against Sam was going well. Sally was relieved that her part was over but Mr. Jeffers reminded them that Sam, being the biological father, had an edge.

The fifteen minute break turned out to be thirty minutes before they were called back to the courtroom. The Judge announced that before any decision could be made there would be one more testimony to be heard. He asked the court clerk to please call the witness. When the courtroom door opened, every eye turned to see who would enter. An audible gasp was heard as they saw the person who would testify. Sally said to her Dad, "Is that Grandma?"

"I think it is," Joe replied, "but she surely looks different."

If it was Grandma, she was dressed in a well tailored black suit, far from the usual housedress and worn apron. Her white hair, neatly pulled into a bun was topped with a smart looking black hat.

"It is Grandma. And that's George walking with her. I recognize him," Joe whispered to Sally.

"Really?"

"Yes, and the young man on her other side must be George's son."

"Dad, do you think our prayers have been answered?" Before he could respond the judge ordered silence in the courtroom. Joe Carter put his arm around Sally, who had tears rolling down her cheeks. He gave her a squeeze as Grandma took her oath.

"Madam, please state your name and address," the court clerk requested.

"My name is Abigail Frances Turner. I live at 220 Turner Street, Riversedge, North Carolina.

"Please state your age."

Mrs. Turner looked at the judge for a long moment and then said, "Judge, isn't this the time someone pops up and says objection because the question is irrelevant?"

There was soft giggling throughout the room. Judge Mathews, with a smile said, "Sustained." And then added, "Mrs. Turner, you may be seated."

Again, the judge had to ask for silence as whispering was rampant when all heard, first of all, Grandma's name, hearing that for the first time and secondly her apparent sense of humor.

Sam stood and audibly said, "What the hell is she doing here?" The judge angrily pounded his gavel as the court clerk approached Sam. "The old lady doesn't know my son. She's a nut case…"

"Sir, either you sit down and control yourself or you're out of here, for good."

Once order was restored, the Judge said, "I will ask this witness questions and then, if either lawyers have further questions, they may do so."

Sam was visibly upset and confused. He had no knowledge that there was a connection between this woman and his son.

Judge Mathews addressed Mrs. Turner. "Please tell this court what you know about the young boy, Peter John Wilson."

"Yes sir." She paused briefly, before she began her story.

CHAPTER EIGHTEEN

You could hear a pin drop as Mrs.Turner, the woman who would forever be referred to as *Grandma,* began to speak. The woman was articulate, confident, soft spoken and composed.

"The hour was late this night in November of last year. I was sitting on my front porch when I saw a little person running across the street towards my house. He ran down the side of the house and into the woods. In the darkness, I couldn't see who it was, so I followed the youngster. The boy was Peter, the young lad I recognized from across the street. He was visibly shaking and crying. We sat on a stone bench and I put my arm around him and held him close. When he finally calmed down, he told me his mommy was crying and his daddy was hitting her."

Gasps filled the room and, "Oh my God," was clearly heard. The judge called for silence and said, "Mrs. Turner, please continue."

"I brought the boy into my house and gave him some warm milk. Then we went out to my front porch where I could plainly see his house across the street. He sat on my lap and we rocked. He fell asleep. When I thought it was safe to bring him home, I awakened him."

"How could you tell it was safe?" The judge asked.

"We had been sitting there for some time and I kept an eye on his house. There had been no activity or lights on for a long time, therefore I thought it would be safe to bring him home."

"I see, please continue."

"I woke him, took him by the hand and we walked across the street to his back door. He quietly entered. I stayed outside until I felt he was safe, then I returned to my house."

"How late at night was this?"

"Probably about three a.m."

"Was this the only time such an event like that happened?"

"Oh no, this happened many times over."

"Many times? How many?"

"Certainly once a week, sometimes more often. Of course Peter was only on Turner Street three nights over the weekend."

"How do you know there were more times this happened?"

"I asked the young lad. He told me, in his words, "it happened a lot." I told him if he was frightened again to come to my front porch. I would be there."

"You stayed up every Friday, Saturday and Sunday nights, watching?"

"I don't sleep well. Even before the first incident, I would sit and rock on the front porch until quite late."

"When, to your knowledge, was the last time Peter went to your front porch because his parents were having problems?"

"The night before his mother took him away, the night before that dreadful accident."

"I have no further questions at this time. If either of the attorneys have any questions, they may ask them now. Thank you, Mrs. Turner for your cooperation."

The Jeffers' attorney said they had no further questions. Sam Wilson's attorney got up from his chair and stood in front of Mrs. Turner. He stared at her for a moment and then asked, "Mrs. Turner do you sit on your front porch to gather gossip from your neighbors all the time?"

Abigail Turner gave him a look not to describe and merely said, "Hardly."

"Is that a yes or a no?" the attorney questioned. At that point the judge asked if he had any pertinent questions.

"Sir, this woman is known in her neighborhood as a strange person and I'm trying to find out what her purpose was in protecting a little boy that she had no knowledge of his parents or the boy himself. Was she just being a busy body or what?" The court room observers became vocally impatient.

The judge banged his gavel and directed his words to the attorney. "This woman is not here to have her character questioned but rather to give testimony as to what she had witnessed." He then turned to Mrs. Turner and thanked her again. Judge Mathews dismissed her.

She rose. George and his son got up and stood on either side escorting her out of the courtroom. Every eye was on them. Joe Carter smiled as they passed by and he thought he saw a glimmer of a smile on Grandma's face too.

The judge said he would talk to the boy Peter, privately. He then would give his decision in one week's time.

"Court adjourned."

CHAPTER NINETEEN

The week flew by, not because of the court custody decision, but rather because four days after Sally's testimony her Dad was leaving to return to his home. Sally hated to see him go. Her Dad had become so much a part of their lives. She would miss him, not to mention the grandchildren. Tommy and Jenny adored him and couldn't understand why he had to leave.

Joe Carter reluctantly packed the rental car. He had a horrible empty feeling after being so much a part of his grandchildren's lives. They truly changed Joe's outlook on his own life. He realized now he had much to live for. As he backed the car out of the driveway, Sally and the kids stood on the porch waving goodbye. Tears streamed down Sally's cheeks. Hidden from view, tears filled Joe Carter's eyes too as he turned off

Turner Street. Turning to go inside, Sally noticed Rose standing on her porch. She apparently had waved goodbye too. Sally knew Rose would miss Joe also. She enjoyed his company.

A few days later, it was time to go back to court for the judge's decision. Sally promised she would call her Dad once the decision was final. Most everyone seemed convinced it would be in favor of the Jeffers, but there was the ever-present uncertainty.

The courtroom wasn't as full as previously. Noticeably, none of Sam's family was there. In fact, when Sally arrived Sam wasn't there either. Leave it to Sam to stroll in at the last moment.

Court was called to order. Judge Mathews was seated. He looked the room over carefully, then called Mrs. Jeffers to the stand. Was the case questionable that they needed more information? Sally wondered.

"How old are you and your husband, Mrs. Jeffers?" the judge asked.

"I am seventy-two years old and my husband is seventy-five." The judge made a note of this, then asked, "Have either of you considered your age concerning Peter's future?"

"Oh, yes sir. The young women seated with my husband and me is our other daughter, Peter's aunt, Annie's younger sister. She has a signed document stating if, for any reason her father or I become incapacitated whatsoever she will legally adopt Peter. "

"Her name again?" the judge asked.

"Martha, Martha Flynn."

"Miss Flynn, will you please come forward." When she was seated the judge reminded her she was still under oath, "Are you married.?"

"Yes sir, and we have a three year old daughter and a four year old son."

"I see." The judge asked several more questions concerning her adopting and bringing up Peter. Martha answered and then handed him a witnessed document stating her adoption plans. It also said this adoption would occur no later than five years from the date on the document or sooner if the need was obvious."

"Where do you reside, Mrs. Flynn.

"I live four doors down from my mother and father."

"Thank you. You may step down." He looked over the courtroom carefully, and then said to the Plaintiff's attorney, "I see your client, Mr. Wilson, is not present in court. Is there an explanation for his absence?"

"I don't know, sir. When I spoke to Mr. Wilson he said he would be here."

"You reminded him?"

"I spoke to him during the week and again last night."

"And he said he would be here?"

"Yes sir, he did."

Judge Mathews spoke briefly to the clerk, who left the courtroom. He returned shortly and told the judge Mr. Wilson was nowhere in the building.

Finally the judge stated, "Mr. Wilson has twenty-four hours to appear in this courtroom, accompanied by his attorney. Failure to do so will relinquish his petition for full custody of his son, Peter James. I apologize to those here present. Court is adjourned until eleven a.m. tomorrow.

It took some time for the courtroom to empty. People lingered, spending time chatting among themselves over this latest development. When the room cleared, the clerk checked for any left articles and went out, locking the courtroom doors.

"Stop! Stop!" someone yelled. "I have to get in there." The clerk pocketed the keys and turned to face the screamer. He recognized Sam Wilson although he didn't let on.

"Sir, the court is close," he said. "The proceedings are over."

"Oh no, they're not. I'm Sam Wilson, the plaintiff in this case. Now, let me in," he demanded."

"I'm sorry, sir, the room has emptied out and the judge has retired to his chambers."

"Well, you just let Mathews know I'm not leaving until I see him."

"If you'd like to sit in the lobby, I'll give him the message," the clerk said, trying to keep his composure. He really wanted to tell him where to go, and it certainly wasn't to see Judge Mathews.

Sam Wilson did get to see the judge. The clerk went to the judge's chambers and told him of his encounter with Mr. Wilson. He said, "That guy thinks the world exists for his wants and his wants only. He wanted that door opened, no matter what."

"He certainly is arrogant," said Judge Matthews. "See if he is still around. If so, bring him to my office. I have a few things to attend to but if he'll wait I'll talk to him."

Sam did wait. In the meantime he contacted his lawyer so he could be present. It was nearly three o'clock before the judge was able to see them. Sam immediately gave all sorts of excuses as to why he'd been late."

The Judge response was, "I will not accept excuses or your belligerent outbursts. Do I make myself clear?" The Judge refused to discuss the case only to say...

Sam blurted. "Look, I couldn't be here this morning, I have other responsibilities, you know."

"As I was saying before I was interrupted...I have studied very carefully all testimonies, and I've had several long talks with your son, Peter. I will give my decision tomorrow morning, whether you, Mr. Wilson, are present or not." Sam's attorney tried desperately to keep Sam quiet, which seldom worked.

By this time the judge had enough of Mr. Wilson, realizing there was no point in continuing to try and talk to him. He stood. "I strongly suggest Mr. Wilson that you be present in court tomorrow morning at eleven. For now, I have nothing further to say. He gave Sam one last look and left the room.

Sam's attorney said, "You sure know how to cook your own goose."

"Don't be so sure."

CHAPTER TWENTY

As Sally drove home from court, she thought about what had transpired, rather what didn't and it was disappointing. She couldn't imagine what Sam was thinking, being so inconsiderate to the court. His love for his son seemed distorted. Sally wondered how much Sam really wanted custody. If he does he isn't going about it smartly.

Rose was surprised to see Sally home before she expected her. "Sally are you alright, tell me what happened."

"I'm fine Rose. That worthless son of gun, Sam didn't show up at court."

"You're kidding? What happens now?"

"Sam is to be in court tomorrow morning for the judge's decision and if he doesn't show up Judge Mathews will give his decision without him.

The Judge was quite angry, which I don't blame him. Sam doesn't seem to care about anyone, only himself."

"Well Sally, feel free to leave the children with me tomorrow too."

"Rose, I can't thank you enough. If you have something else to do, please don't let me stop you. The decision will be made with or without me. The Jeffers can let me know the outcome."

"Don't be silly, I wouldn't think of it. You should be there." Sally thanked Rose again and took the children home for their naps. She no sooner got them settled when the phone rang. It was her Dad.

Sally told her father what happened in court and he too was disappointed. "You know, Sal, it seems Sam might have spoiled any chance for getting custody."

"Let's hope." Sally assured her Dad she would call him with the news.

At precisely eleven the next morning, Judge Mathews called the courtroom to order. Both Plaintiff and Respondent were present.

There was complete silence as Judge Mathews began, "In family court, I always find these decisions difficult as far as the adults are concerned. However, I am not here to be overly concerned with adults. My ONLY concern is the involved child's welfare. I have spoken to Peter several times and it has been a difficult time for him. His recent loss of his Mother must be taken into consideration. It was obvious he had a close relationship with her. I have seriously taken all testimony and facts under advisement and have come to the only conclusion possible. Therefore, my decision in this case, Wilson vs. Jeffers, is to award full custody to Mildred and Richard Jeffers.

Before the judge could finish there was a round of applause. He pounded the gavel for silence and continued. "Peter's grandparents will have full custody and Mr. Wilson is granted accompanied visitation rights until such time the court is convinced Mr. Wilson proves himself to be a responsible parent."

Sam jumped up, ranting, "You have no right to do this." His lawyer tried to calm him and urged him to be quiet. The Judge again called for order. The clerk approached Sam, ready to remove him from the room unless he quieted down.

He stood and again yelled, "This isn't over. I will, what do you call it, appeal, that's it." By this time, two officers were behind him ready to withdraw him from the room.

"You have a right to do so, Mr. Wilson." Judge Mathews gavel came down hard. This hearing is adjourned." He rose from his chair and left. Again applause broke out.

Sally couldn't wait to get home to call her Dad with the good news. Before she left court she congratulated the Jeffers. "I'm so happy for you but most of all for Peter. Mr. Jeffers gave Sally a hug, "Thanks to you and your wonderful father."

"I don't know how it happened but I'm sure glad it did," Sally said smiling, "What convinced Grandma, excuse me I guess I should say Mrs. Turner. Anyway what made her come to court I don't know, but we do know how much she cared for Peter."

"Yes that's for sure," Mr. Jeffers agreed.

By this time Mrs. Jeffers and Annie's sister, Martha joined them, "Mrs. Turner gave such a touching testimony and you are right, it was obvious how much she cares for Peter."

"Is Peter alright?" Does he understand what's going on?" Sally asked.

"That's hard to say, but Judge Mathews made it easy for him, I think." Martha replied.

"How so?"

"Peter saw the judge twice. My father took him first and I took him the last time. Judge Mathews saw him alone for over an hour both times. My father and I agree the judge knows how to handle these situations and definitely knows how to talk to children. Peter was so at ease after being with him."

"Yes Martha, and each time after Peter talked with judge he came out smiling," Mr. Jeffers added.

"Peter didn't say much as to what they talked about, but did say he thought the man was real nice." Martha smiled.

They chatted a few minutes more before they said their goodbyes, promising to keep in touch. Sally headed for home, relieved this was behind them now. Peering out the front window, Rose waited anxiously. She had been watching the children and was becoming very attached to them.

Sally no sooner was in the door, hugged the children and Rose saying, "We won. Peter will stay with his grandparents."

"That's great news. Was Grandma there?" Rose wondered

"No, as a matter of fact she wasn't, but I'm sure she knows." Sally thought for a moment then turned to Rose and asked, "Rose would you mind staying with the children another few minutes while I run down to Grandma's house just to be sure she does know. I'll only be a minute."

CHAPTER TWENTY-ONE

Sally's Dad was delighted to hear the verdict favored the Jeffers and that Peter would be able to live with his grandparents. He said it many times during their telephone conversation. "Grandma sure came through for Peter, didn't she?"

"Yeah, she did," Sally answered.

"What's with you, you almost sound disappointed?"

"Of course I'm not, it's just I thought maybe she would change after the hearing."

"Maybe she will. Time will tell."

"I don't think so. When I got home after the hearing I walked down to her house to make sure she had heard the good news. I saw her sitting on the front porch so I knew she saw me. By the time I got to her front stoop she was going in her front door."

"Sally, you don't know why she went inside, there could have been any number of reasons."

"Maybe so, I guess I was hoping Mrs. Turner wouldn't go back to being Grandma. I'm sure she saw me and no doubt she knew the verdict was in. I thought she would want to know right away."

"Sally, let it go. She is what she is and I doubt anything will change her. She probably heard the news from someone else, maybe even from George."

"Oh, she just makes me mad."

"Forget it Sal," her Dad said. They continued talking about Grandma for some time, then their conversation turned to Tom's coming home and the future plans they were making. Joe Carter tried not to let on how much he missed being with Sally and the children. He too, like Sally, was counting the days until Tom's return. With her husband home it might make the possibility of their moving closer, a reality.

With the arrival of spring, Sally spent part of her time outside with the kids and in her garden. Not long ago Tommy had spent a day at the Jeffers with Peter. While there he found out Peter was no longer using training wheels on his bike which meant Tommy wouldn't be happy until his were off.

Needless to say, Sally spent time running along his side holding the bike upright. Fortunately, it didn't take long before Tommy was riding by himself, sporting several scraped knees.

One afternoon Mr. Jeffers dropped Peter and his bike off so the boys could have a play day together. The two of them had a great time riding up and down the sidewalks of Turner Street, with Sally keeping a sharp eye on them. She watched, at one point, as they were headed up the street towards Grandma's house. Grandma was sitting on her porch. As soon as Peter saw her, he dropped his bike and ran up the steps. Tommy followed close behind. Sally wondered if Grandma would retreat inside the house. She didn't. She welcomed Peter with a big hug as well as one for Tommy. They both stood in front of her rocking chair chatting away. Sally would have loved to have heard their conversation. They weren't there long before a man came out of the house with a tray of cookies. Sally wondered if that was George. She never saw him or anyone for that matter there during the day. The boys were there for awhile before they headed home, with little bags tied to their handlebars.

"Mommy look what the nice lady gave us, a whole bag of cookies," Tommy yelled excitedly.

"Well, aren't you the lucky boys." Sally smiled, she wanted to ask questions but decided it was best to let well enough alone.

A few days later, Sally noticed a car in front of Grandma's house. Anything out of the ordinary at Grandma's was always noticed. Rose stopped by, "Hey what do you think about the old lady having company?"

"I guess it's unusual but why not?"

"Let me tell you, I've lived here for a lot of years and I've never seen a parked car in front of that woman's house."

"Well then, it is unusual," Sally said wanting to end that conversation.

"I tell you, it is."

"Rose, do you really dislike the woman that much?" Sally asked.

Rose was indignant at the suggestion. "Why I never said I didn't like the woman. You have to admit,

Sally, she is different and certainly not friendly.

"I know, but as my Dad would say, she has a reason for her actions that we don't know and Dad is right because it's none of our business."

"No matter, but it is strange to see a car in front of her house, which never happened before."

Sally thought to herself, I give up. However, as time passed, she noted there was a car in front of Grandma's every day, plus the fact she wasn't sitting on her front porch as often. It puzzled Sally and the thought crossed her mind that something might be wrong or possibly Grandma was sick. Sally had more important things though to think about. The night before she had received a phone call from Tom and he would be arriving in the states the end of May. That was almost a month earlier than expected and only four weeks away. Just thinking that Tom would be home soon made everything else less important.

But Sally sat on her porch after the day's chores were done and the children were asleep. All was quiet on Turner Street, but not at Grandma's house. It looked like every light in the house was on. Sally had a strong feeling something was very wrong. She would have to drop by Grandma's house tomorrow and make sure she was alright.

CHAPTER TWENTY-TWO

One evening as Sally was talking on the phone with her Dad, she told him, "I'm sure Grandma is sick, we never see her on her front porch."

"Really, have you been able to talk to anyone about her?"

"No, Dad, getting ready for Tom's homecoming, keeping an eye on Tommy's bike riding, Jenny not happy in the back yard without Tommy. Oh, I shouldn't be complaining." Sally knew she was making excuses which made her even more upset. She truly cared about Grandma and felt she should have made time to check on her.

Her Dad was also concerned, but more so about his daughter. "Take it easy honey, you have a lot on your plate these days. Next week Tom will be home and all will be well, I promise,"

'I can't wait Dad. Every time I think about him my heart skips a beat. I don't mean to sound unconcerned about Grandma though."

"I know that." Her father's words were comforting. She realized how good it was to have him in her life again and wanted him nearby.

"When are you coming?" Sally asked.

"Listen, you and Tom should have time for yourselves before you're ready to see me."

"Well, don't wait long. We've plans to make together." They talked a while longer. When Sally hung up she suddenly felt guilty about not checking on Grandma.

That afternoon while Tommy was bike riding, Sally wasn't far behind with Jenny in her stroller. As they approached Grandma's house she noticed several people sitting on the front porch, as well as several cars parked in front. She recognized

George as he came to the top of the stoop. Sally called Tommy to turn around as George was descending the steps.

"George," Sally called.

"Hi there," George said recognizing her.

"Could I speak to you for a moment?"

"Why sure."

"George, how is your aunt? I haven't seen her outside in a while."

"I know," he hesitated. "She is failing."

"You mean sick?"

"Yes, Ma'am, really bad."

"I'm so sorry. What can I do?"

"I wish I could change the situation but nobody can help anymore."

As Sally turned to leave she looked up on the porch. She was saying, "Please, if I can do anything please let me know, anything at all." Walking away she again glanced at the people sitting on the porch. This time she was sure. One was Judge Mathews.

As she approached her house Rose met her, "What in the world is going on here? That woman never had any visitors and now look at all those cars..."

"Rose, Rose," Sally interrupted "that woman, as you call her, is very sick."

"I didn't know she knew a soul, or that anyone would even care."

"Rose, let's not go into that again. I have to run now. I'll see you later." Sally's anger was building inside of her. It bothered her that Rose didn't skip a beat after hearing Grandma was sick. She got the kids settled in the back yard and immediately called her Dad. "Dad I had to call. Grandma is very ill."

"You thought so. Who did you talk to?"

"George. Guess who else was sitting on the porch that we know?"

"Tell me." Her Dad laughed, knowing full well she would.

"Aren't you the funny one?"

"Sorry honey, tell me."

"Judge Mathews."

"That is interesting for the Judge to be there. I wonder what his connection is with Grandma? What did George say was Grandma's problem?"

"He didn't really. All he said was she was very sick and failing. It sounded like she's beyond any help."

"Whatever her illness is, it must have affected Grandma rather quickly. She looked great at the hearing, certainly not sick." Joe recalled.

"I thought so too. George kind of sounded like she had been ill for some time."

Every day now the cars keep coming and it goes on all day. I guess Dad, there's a lot we don't' know about Abigail Turner." Sally hesitated before adding, "You know Dad I still can't stop calling her Grandma."

He agreed. "Sally, let me know what's going on. Okay?"

Before hanging up, Sally said, "I love you Dad. I'll keep you posted."

Every day Sally got up at the crack of dawn to make a couple of cookie trays. She brought them to Grandma's and left them on her front porch. After three days of delivering the cookies a woman rang Sally's doorbell. When Sally answered the door she didn't recognize the lady, but she did recognize her cookie platters.

"Hi, I'm Aunt Abby's niece, George's wife." the woman said handing the platters to Sally.

"Oh yes, come in."

"No, I just came to return your plates and to thank you. Your cookies were delicious and very much appreciated."

How is Gran...," Sally said but started over. "How is your aunt doing?"

"There hasn't been any significant change the last few days but she is very weak. I really think the end is near."

CHAPTER TWENTY-THREE

The day or better put, the night finally arrived when Tom came home. It was seven-thirty in the evening and Sally was getting the children ready for bed. They had finished their baths and Sally was drying off Jenny while Tommy was getting his p-jays on in the hall.

"Mommy," Tommy yelled, "I hear a robber coming in the front door."

"Don't be a silly boy."

Tommy yelled louder, "Hey, it's Daddy." Tom climbed the stairs two by two and grabbed his son in his arms. At the same time, Sally grabbed Jenny, bath towel and all and ran into the hallway. With children in their arms there was much kissing and hugging for everyone. Excitement abound. It was well passed the children's bedtime before they were finally settled in their beds.

"Have you eaten?" Sally asked as she and Tom went back downstairs.

"I grabbed a hot dog before leaving the base but a good cup of coffee would be great." When they got to the bottom of the staircase Tom took Sally in his arms and pressed her body against his. "Sally, I love you," he whispered in her ear. "I've dreamed of this moment for months." They never did have a cup of coffee that night.

The next morning Tom was the first up, dressed and downstairs. He unpacked the rental car and got the coffee maker perking before Tommy was at his side, followed by Sally carrying Jenny. She put Jenny in the highchair, flung her arms up in the air and said, "We're all together again and Daddy is here to stay." She kissed her children and gave a huge hug and kiss to her husband followed by, "Thank God."

The next few days were filled with love making, play and laughter in the Lester home. Sally, wearing a constant smile, couldn't be happier. And it didn't take young Tommy any time to reconnect with his Dad. They were good pals. It did take little longer for Jenny to warm up to Tom, but in no time, she had her Daddy wrapped around her finger and he loved it.

Tom was well aware of the happenings on Turner Street during the time he was away. There were his frequent phone calls home and of course Sally's daily letters. He understood Sally's concerns about Grandma along with the visitors and cars coming and going, as well as Sally's cookies going and platters coming back. Tom admired Sally and her thoughtfulness and was proud of how deeply she cared for others.

He wasn't home long before he went to the real estate agency where

Tom and Sally leased their house on Turner Street. The lease was up in three months and Tom wanted to see if they could shorten the time by a month. He, as well as Sally, and not to mention Joe Carter, all wanted and were anxious to get their lives settled in one place. Their plans to go north to be near Joe were still what they wanted for themselves and the children. The agent was not too cooperative, but said he would have to talk to the owner and see what he wanted. He would let them know.

On his way back, going down Turner Street was like being in a city traffic jam. Cars were parked all over the place, some three deep from the curb. Tom knew it was all people visiting at Grandma's house. He found out as soon as he reached home that Grandma had died the night before and evidently was being waked in her home. Sally was waiting on the front porch and was visibly upset as she told Tom. He put his arms around her and said, "I know Sally, even though you didn't have the opportunity to really get to know Grandma, you truly cared about her and you know, I think she cared about you too."

"I wish I had known her better. For some reason I really wanted to know her. I think, Tom, she was a remarkable lady at one time. But we do have good news, I called Dad and he's flying here tonight. He cared too."

"That's great, he should be here. What say we take the kids to the airport? They've never seen a plane up close. Tommy would love it and Jenny loves everything."

"That sounds like a good idea, Tom. I'm so glad you're home." Sally put her arms around him.

Joe Carter's plane was due at six twenty-five that evening. He had planned on renting a car but was thrilled to see his family waiting for him. They stopped for a bite to eat before returning to Turner Street. When they got there, it still was a maze of cars all over the street and crowds of people milling around outside on Grandma's front porch and the sidewalk.

When the children were put to bed, the three adults sat outside on the porch. It was a beautiful balmy night. They talked about their future plans as they watched in wonderment at the cars finally leaving the street. All was quiet. However, Grandma's house had many lights shining through its windows.

Their silence was broken when Rose appeared coming up the front steps saying, "Isn't this unbelievable?" Then she turned and saw Joe. "Oh, my heavens, when did you get here? You must have just arrived. You weren't here yesterday. It's so good to see you."

"I told you she had a crush on Dad," Sally whispered to Tom. They sat out there for a few minutes longer but since their peace and quiet had been broken, Sally said, "It's been a long day so you'll have to excuse us." She took Tom's hand and headed towards the door.

Joe was still sitting. Rose saw the emptied rocker next to him and started to sit. Joe jumped up, "Oh yes, yes you'll have to excuse me also, long trip you know. I'm really tired."

Rose, visually disappointed said, "Of course, but I'll see you tomorrow."

"Tomorrow. Yes of course, goodnight Rose."

CHAPTER TWENTY-FOUR

Joe was first up the next morning. He made the coffee, got a cup and went outside on the porch to read the paper. Although the temperature was nearing the eighties, there was a nice breeze. When he put his coffee on the table he found another returned cookie platter with a sealed envelope addressed to The Lester Family. He brought both inside the house.

Turner Street was quiet with not a soul to be seen. He looked at his watch. "Oh my, it's only six thirty, no wonder there's no one around."

He finished his coffee and was about to get a second cup when Tom came outside with his cup and the coffee pot. "I think it's going to be a hot one today," Tom said as he poured the coffee and sat down.

"Right now we have a little breeze. It's pretty nice here on the porch," Joe replied. The two men chatted away as always enjoying each other's company. Then Joe remembered. "I forgot, that platter on the hallway table has an envelope for you guys. They both were out here on the table when I first came out."

"Okay, thanks. It must be a thank you note for Sally's cookies."

The screen door opened and Tommy rushed out with Sally right behind, carrying Jenny. "Good morning early birds," Sally said with a smile. Tommy jumped up on his Dad's lap and Joe got up so Sally could sit down. Instead, Sally gave Jenny to her grandfather and said, "You sit Dad and I'll go inside and get our breakfast."

"What's on the menu?" Tom asked

"Well you'll have to go downtown to the diner and find out."

"We got told," Joe said. Sally laughed as she went inside.

She was only there for a moment when she came back out with the envelope she just opened. "My God this is amazing."

"Well, they should thank you," Tom noted.

"This isn't a thank you, Tom. Here, read it."

Tom took the engraved invitation and read it, "Wow."

"Read it out loud," Sally asked.

"Okay, it reads:

On Saturday, June Fifth
You are invited
To the Funeral and Burial Services
In Celebration of the Life of
Abigail F. Turner
At four o'clock in the afternoon
A reception will follow the burial

"And at the bottom, it reads,"

Invitation Required

"That's really something," Joe commented. "I have a feeling this is going to be quite a farewell. It certainly will be interesting. I think we'll learn a lot more about Abigail Turner."

He no sooner finished his sentence when young Tommy said, "Hey, look at those big, big trucks." Indeed there were two big trucks starting to back into the side yard of Grandma's house.

"Are they moving vans?" Sally asked.

"I don't think so. There aren't any markings on the sides of the trucks," Tom answered.

"Well, gentlemen, I think I better get breakfast started. Dad, I'll take Jenny and get her settled in her high chair with some Cheerios."

"I'll help in a minute," Tom offered.

At the breakfast table the conversation was about the goings on at Grandma's. They watched the trucks unload and it appeared to be the makings of a very large tent and countless folding chairs.

"This isn't only going to be a ceremony but an event from the looks of things," Tom remarked.

"I think you're right, although it's certainly unlike Grandma herself. At least the way she lived here on Turner Street," Sally said.

"I guess we're about to find a lot about this lady that we couldn't have imagined," Joe thought out loud. "But let's get on with today, so how about a trip to the park, Tommy?"

That was met with hurrahs and clapping of hands from both young ones. The plan was for Tom and Joe to take the kids to the park and Sally would get done whatever was needed to do at home. Not to completely leave Sally out, they decided to bring lunch home for all. Everyone agreed and they were on their way. Sally started to make more cookies for Grandma's household. Tom yelled back to Sally as they were leaving, "Don't forget to save some of those chocolate chip cookies for us."

Sally went about baking and doing her household chores, while the men and children were having fun in the park. When they returned, Joe and Tom were each carrying a sleeping child, which they brought upstairs to their beds. "We had a great time and got the kids something to eat while we had the deli make up our lunch. How was your morning, honey?" Tom asked as he and Joe came into the kitchen.

"It's amazing how much I got done with no kids under foot, thanks to you guys."

"Our pleasure," Tom bowed.

"I'm sure you saw the humongous tent in Grandma's back yard. Isn't that something? They had and remarked that it looked like there were over one hundred chairs. They went outside to have their lunch on the porch and watched all the activity at Grandma's. Eating their chocolate chip cookies, Sally mentioned she hadn't had a chance to bring them down the street.

"Sally, don't bother, I'll deliver them now." Joe picked up the platter and was on his way.

CHAPTER TWENTY-FIVE

Joe didn't leave the cookies on Grandma's front porch fearing they'd melt in the heat, so he rang the doorbell. A man opened the door immediately, "Oh my, more cookies. I can't tell you how much we appreciate them."

As Joe handed him the cookies, he realized it was George. "Hi George, I'm Joe Carter."

"Of course, I remember you."

"I'm sorry to hear of Grandma's death. Excuse me, I mean Mrs. Turner."

"No matter, but thank you. I'm going to miss the ole gal. Hey have you a minute?"

"Sure."

"Sit with me for a few here on the porch. I'll be right out. I better put these cookies away." He disappeared,, then came back carrying two glasses of lemonade. "I hope you and your family will be here tomorrow."

"Certainly, we will. My daughter Sally had a special fondness for your aunt."

"As well as Aunt Abby did for her."

"We didn't realize she was sick. Sally told me she looked terrific at the hearing,"

"Yes, she did. She actually surprised us all, but then she always had a special inner strength."

"We have you to thank for talking her into testifying."

"Oh no, I didn't talk her into anything. It was Judge Mathews."

"Judge Mathews? How did he know her and what's more, she even knew young Peter?" Joe was really puzzled at this point.

"Aunt Abby called the judge. I think it was shortly after you sent her the note explaining the need for her to testify. The judge and she are long time good friends."

"Really?"

"That's right. She told Judge Mathews what she knew about the young boy. The judge asked her to come to court to tell her story. As you know, Aunt Abby rarely went anywhere these days."

"She didn't want to go to court?"

"Right, but the judge explained how important it was for him to hear everything so he could make the right decision for Peter."

"And she finally agreed?"

"Yes. I understand it took a bit of persuasion before she did. My son and I brought her to court. She was put in an ante-room but able to hear what was going on in the hearing. When she was called to testify she related what had happened concerning Peter. She answered questions posed by the attorneys and was allowed to leave immediately after."

"I'll be darned," Joe commented, "that's interesting."

"I think your note was really what persuaded her more than anything. I found it in her desk the other day. Your words were strong and effective. I really think it did the trick."

"No matter, she saved little Peter's future." The two men talked for a few minutes. Shortly after a woman came outside to tell George he had a phone call.

George stood and as he was entering the house he said, "Joe this is my wife, Marion. We'll talk again."

"Hello, how nice to meet you." Joe said.

"Yes, I met your lovely daughter. She's a sweetie making all those delicious cookies."

"I agree, she is lovely," Joe said as he went down the stairs. "Thank you." As Joe started walking to the Lester's he felt disappointed his talk with George was cut short. The more he heard about Abigail Turner the more interested he became. Joe wasn't half way down the block when he heard George call him. As he was walking towards Joe he said, "Tell your son-in-law not to worry about breaking the lease. That call was from the realtor. They can leave whenever necessary or stay as long as they wish. They don't have to worry about any lease."

Joe, not quite sure what he was talking about said, "Sure. I'll tell them."

Sally and Tom were sitting in the back yard when Joe returned. Sally told him his sandwich was in the fridge and to come out and join them.

"I take it the angels are still taking a nap?"

"Yes, they were really wiped out after our jaunt in the park," Tom reported.

Then Sally said, "You were gone longer than we thought, so we ate without you. How are things at Grandma's?"

"Well it seems every minute we learn more about Grandma. She really is something, so much more than the recluse we thought." Joe then told them about Grandma's long-time friendship with the judge.

Sally interrupted. "That's why he was sitting on the porch the other day."

"I guess so," and he continued telling them how she was convinced to give testimony in court. Like Joe, they were amazed. "Oh by the way, George said to tell you not to worry about your lease, you can leave or stay, whatever you want to do. What's that all about?"

"How in the world does George know about that? I asked a realtor in town."

"I have no idea, Tom. George got a phone call and came out and told me to give you the message."

"And we thought Grandma was strange." Sally remarked

CHAPTER TWENTY-SIX

The night before the funeral Joe Carter went outside to sit on the porch. For whatever reason, he didn't know why, he was having difficulty sleeping. It was a beautiful moonlit night. He was enjoying a beer and quiet time. One of things he was concerned about was that Sally and Tom would make the right decision about their move. As much as he wanted them close to him, it was more important they be happy.

It was late and Turner Street was asleep except for Grandma's house which was lit up like a Christmas tree. He doubted there wasn't a room that didn't have lights on. Suddenly, Joe saw a figure walking through the darkness. As the person approached the Lester's house, Joe thought it looked like George. "George, is that you?" He asked.

"Woo, who are you?"

"I'm sorry if I frightened you. It's Joe," he said as he came down the steps.

"I didn't expect to meet up with anyone this time of night."

"I was having trouble sleeping and came outside. I didn't want to disturb my sleeping family," Joe explained.

"I had to get out of the house. Everyone is trying to decide how to manage tomorrow's services and each one has a different idea. I don't want to get in the middle of that mess. Just tell me what to do and I'll do it...Amen."

"I guess it could get pretty hectic. Hey, why don't you come up on the porch and have a beer with me."

"Now that's an idea I can go along with, no problem."

Joe brought out two beers and the men sat in silence for a few minutes. It seemed both were where they wanted to be at that moment. Joe broke the silence. "You know George, it amazes me your family is going through all this to celebrate your aunt's life and she didn't want to celebrate it herself."

"I can understand your thinking but you didn't know the real Abby. Her life ended here, but there was much more to her life."

"How long did she live on Turner Street?" Joe asked.

"Thirty years, or so. I was just a kid when she moved here."

"And all these years she has been, more or less, a recluse?"

"I guess you could say that, at least to those who didn't really know her. Behind those closed doors she wasn't the woman you knew sitting on her front porch."

They sat in silence for a few minutes. George seemed content and deep in thought. Joe didn't want to disturb him. He got two more beers and George said, "This will have to be my last. You know tomorrow I have to be prim and proper in front of all Riversedge's finest and those beyond." Joe had a feeling he would rather have more beers than perform in front of Riversedge's elite. "You know Joe, sitting here talking about Aunt Abby brings back so many wonderful memories. She really was quite the lady and I'm sorry you guys didn't get to know what she was really like."

"I'm sorry too. Tell me a little about her, if you don't mind."

George sat with his hands folded, rocking back and forth, staring into space deep in thought. "That, my friend, would take months to tell, but I'll try to give you some of the highlights. She was born on a farm, her parents were struggling farmers. They didn't have much, but that didn't matter. My Dad, her brother and a sister who died early on...were her only siblings. They were a happy, hardworking family. I'm told Abby was a spirited child, full of fun, seldom sat down and always helping someone. My Dad would say she was full of vim and vigor."

"Is your Dad still alive?" Joe asked.

"No, he died four years ago. He had a stroke some years back and never was the same, except for his caring about Abby. His visits here were the highlight of his life, especially after my Mom died. I always came with him so it wasn't long before our visits became the highpoint of my life, too."

"So this house was once a happy place where Grandma welcomed visitors?"

"She and her son moved here a few months after her husband, Uncle Jim died."

"I didn't know she had any children."

"Yes. He was the joy of her life. It might interest you to know his name was Peter...Peter James."

"That is interesting and maybe it explains her fondness for young Peter Wilson."

"I think you're right. Aunt Abby's Peter became very ill when he was...I think he was about seven years old. Several months later he died. Life was never the same for Aunt Abby. Losing

Uncle Jim and then Peter was too much for her to bear. It was almost like she wished she could die, too. Whatever, she never was the same again. It was as if she got too close to people they would leave her."

"Life sure has strange twists." Joe commented and then asked, "You seemed to have had a close relationship with her, no?"

"I never stopped coming, but always in the dark through the back door. That was the way she wanted it. I don't think she wanted the outside world to know she cared about anybody but let me tell you she cared. I begged her to come to my wedding. She wouldn't but made arrangements for the church and the reception hall to be decked in beautiful flowers. She told me when I looked at the flowers I would know she was there and she loved me."

"So she did have some contact with the outside world."

"Oh yes, but only by telephone. She knew many people and had many friends.

She had been part of their lives. For most, she was a very important part. She used the phone only to be sure her family and friends were well, safe and in need of nothing. When you saw her sitting on the front porch, she wasn't wondering what was going on the neighborhood, she sat there dreaming of what could have been and wondered why it wasn't God's plan."

"She certainly was quite the lady. I'm sorry we didn't have the opportunity to know her better," Joe commented. Again they sat in silence nourishing their own thoughts.

A few moments later George stood, "I see most of Abby's windows are dark now. That must mean plans are complete and all is well. So I think I will say goodnight, my friend. Thank you for caring." Joe walked a short way with George, stopped, shook his hand and both went their separate ways.

CHAPTER TWENTY-SEVEN

At nine a.m. Mrs. Jeffers daughter, Martha arrived at the Lester's to pick up Tommy and Jenny. Peter came running up the front stoop calling, "Tommy come on, you're coming to my Aunt Martha's. Wait until you see her neat pool." Sally had the kids packed, swimsuits and all, ready to go. The Jeffers would be coming to the funeral so Martha and her husband volunteered to watch all the children.

They no sooner turned off Turner Street when a caravan of small trucks entered. There were florists, caterers, plus several unmarked trucks. The Lesters and Joe Carter sat on the front porch watching the parade and the multitude of people setting up. "If you look around the neighborhood, practically everyone living on the street is watching the show," Tom remarked and added, "This should by quite an occasion this afternoon."

"Yes. Abigail Turner certainly touched many people's lives for her family to be expecting so many people to attend her funeral," Joe said.

"Doesn't it seem so contrary to what we found her to be?" Sally asked and they all agreed.

Joe then told them about his encounter with George the night before.

"When last night?" Sally interrupted.

"It was late. I guess around twelve-thirty. I had trouble sleeping so I came out here and that's when I spotted George walking.

"He was walking at that time of night?" Sally asked.

"Yes, he wanted out of the confusion at Grandma's house. We sat out here, had a couple of beers, but what George had to tell about Grandma is what I wanted you to know." Then he related the fascinating story of Aunt Abby and who she really was. Sally and Tom were amazed.

The three sat on the porch watching the goings on. They mostly enjoyed being together.

While sitting there, Joe showed them several brochures of communities located close to his home up north. They spread them out on the table when Joe said, "You know what probably would be your best plan to help you make your decision?"

"What's that Dad?" Sally asked.

"You come north and stay with me. You'd be able to take your time and get a close look at these places. You know I'm a star babysitter."

"That probably would be a smart thing to do," Tom agreed. The three started making serious plans about moving where and when. As the men continued to talk Sally made and brought out lunch.

Rose came up on the porch. It was obvious she wasn't happy with the fact the Lesters were moving plus she wasn't invited to the burial. But she was unusually quiet about it. "Oh, I didn't realize you were eating, I'll come back later."

"Don't be silly, join us. We're having sandwiches and there's plenty."

"I've already had lunch so I'll run along," Rose said going down the steps.

"You haven't forgotten dinner tomorrow night?" Sally called.

"No, I'll be there. I'm looking forward to it."

When Rose was out of earshot, Sally said, "I think Grandma touched Rose, too."

By one o'clock in the afternoon they were amazed at the transformation of Grandma's yard. Under the huge tent over one hundred chairs were arranged in rows. A raised platform with a podium complete with a sound system throughout had been installed. One side of the platform was set up for musicians and flowers, of every color, covered the stage. A backdrop of blue drapes hung behind the platform with two large pictures hanging; one of a beautiful young Abby, the other of her handsome husband, Jim. It was clear to see they must have been a fantastic couple. A red velvet roping encircled the entire tent area.

By three o'clock cars started to arrive. A group of young men, valets, dressed in white shirts and tie with black trousers, were in place to park cars in a lot around the corner. Every guest was greeted by men who checked their invitations and escorted them to the tent. Ushers took them to their seats. Soft music was played in the background by the musicians. It was equal to a Hollywood production.

At four o'clock sharp, every seat was occupied and the minister approached the podium. Prayers were said and one by one men and women of every walk of life eulogized Abby. They told of Abby's remarkable kindnesses, her charity to all, her support of desegregation before the word was even known. They talked about how she and her husband, Jim, built communities in Riversedge and other nearby towns.

A woman with a beautiful voice sang "Amazing Grace". Then the minister approached the podium again. "This land and house was Abby and Jim's first home. It was the first of many homes they were to live in. Abby moved back here after her beloved husband, Jim was killed in the horrific construction accident, most of us remember. This land and house became a sacred place for Abby especially after her only child, Peter James died. It was her place to grieve and remember and to be alone. She found it impossible to share her grief with the exception of a chosen few. Yet here we all are to celebrate Abby's life at her very private place. There is no place Abby Turner would rather be even in death. The minister announced the burial would take place in Abby's woods next to her adored son, Peter. He added, "Only immediate family will attend the burial."

George, carrying Abby's urn, led the procession of family members on a red carpet placed from the tent to the woods. There wasn't a dry eye in the tent. In the distance a harp and violin could be heard. No one made a sound nor moved. It was several minutes before the harp and violin stopped. People began to stand and move around.

The musicians on the podium began to play again. In short order, the entire tent changed in appearance. Long tables were put along one side where food was placed, unbelievable amounts of food of every variation imaginable. With what seemed like magic, tables and chairs were set up without disturbing any guests. Place settings were made with floral centerpieces on each table. It couldn't have been more than ten minutes when everything was in place. Everyone was asked to take their seats. The music stopped, the minister stood to say the blessing while the harp and violin were again heard in the distance.

Grandma had done it again; not seen but you knew she was there.

CPSIA information can be obtained at www.ICGtesting.com
Printed in the USA
LVOW101333120313

323604LV00001B/1/P